W9-ATM-013

I Do

I Do

A GUIDE TO CREATING YOUR OWN
UNIQUE WEDDING CEREMONY

Sydney Barbara Metrick

ILLUSTRATED BY TERRY HATCHER

CELESTIAL ARTS
BERKELEY, CALIFORNIA

Poem III of "Twenty One Love Poems" from *The Dream of Common Language, Poems 1974–1977* by Adrienne Rich. Copyright © 1978 by W. W. Norton & Company, Inc. Reprinted by kind permission of the author and W. W. Norton & Company, Inc.

"Reprise" from *VERSUS* by Ogden Nash. Copyright © 1947 by Ogden Nash. Reprinted by kind permission of Little, Brown and Company.

Excerpt from *Notes on Love and Courage* by Hugh Prather. Copyright © 1977 by Hugh Prather. Reprinted by kind permission of Bantam, Doubleday, Dell Publishing Group, Inc.

"Wreath for a Bridal" from *The Collected Poems of Sylvia Plath*, edited by Ted Hughes. Copyright © 1956 by Ted Hughes. Reprinted by kind permission of HarperCollins Publishers, Inc.

Excerpt from "Little Gidding" from *Four Quartets* by T. S. Eliot. Copyright © 1943 by T. S. Eliot and renewed 1971 by Esme Valerie Eliot. Reprinted by kind permission of Harcourt Brace Jovanovich, Inc.

"Come Rain or Come Shine" (Johnny Mercer, Harold Arlen) © 1946 (Renewed) Chappell & Co. All Rights Reserved. Used By Permission.

Copyright © 1992 by Sydney Barbara Metrick. All rights reserved.
No part of this book may be reproduced in any form, except for
brief review, without the written permission of the publisher.
For information write: Celestial Arts Publishing,
Post Office Box 7123, Berkeley, California 94707.

Text and cover design by Sarah Levin
Illustrations by Terry Hatcher
Typesetting by Ann Flanagan Typography

FIRST CELESTIAL ARTS PRINTING 1992

Library of Congress Cataloging-in-Publication Data

Metrick, Sydney Barbara, 1947–
    I do : a guide to creating your own wedding ceremony /
    Sydney Metrick ; illustrated by Terry Hatcher.
        p.   cm.
    Includes bibliographical references.
    ISBN 0-89087-679-7
    1. Marriage service—United States.   I. Title.
HQ745.M84   1992
392'.5'0973—dc20   92-23758
                                          CIP

Printed in the United States of America

2   3   4   5   6   7   8   9   10   /   97   96   95   94   93

Acknowledgments

I would like to give special thanks to all those who offered inspiration and support: Allen and Bärbel Young, Deborah Knighton-Garcha, Sharon Lewis, John Fleer, Danny Bitker, Francis Dreher and Hilda Goldman, Linda Penzur, Sandy Dibbel-Hope, Sherrill Dana, Shaun McElhannon, Tim and Tryntje, Christine and Kelly, Ryan and Corrina, Melanie and Stephan Hofman, and Chris Orr. And I want to extend my heartfelt appreciation to Don Hausler, librarian at the Lakeview branch of the Oakland Public Library.

Dedication

I would like to dedicate this book to the memory of the first man I ever wanted to marry—my dad, George Metrick.

Contents

Love

Love is

Love is one

One has love within one

And lovers

when in love

give love

and grow love

and live love

and know love

uncover

discover

'till finally lovers

are one

S. B. Metrick

Introduction

Marriage versus Wedding— Do You Know the Difference?

When two people decide they are going to marry, numerous feelings are evoked. They first experience happiness and a sense of possibility, excitement, perhaps feelings of glowing warmth and fulfillment. Then as talk of the ceremony comes around that initial joyous spirit is likely to be replaced by questions and complications as a deluge of details begs for attention. Planning a wedding is a complex and demanding process. Preparing for a wedding may bring up issues that can, in many ways, be a test for the marriage.

It is helpful to think about the difference between a marriage and a wedding. *Marriage* indicates the pledge of loyalty and faithfulness that two people make to each other. *Wedding* more commonly refers to the ceremony that publicly represents this promise. Let's look first at the idea of marriage.

Marriage

Currently in our culture, a marriage between two people is typically based on a love, understanding, and acceptance these people have for and with each other. It is no longer common for marriages to be arranged. In times past there were social forces such as considerations of blood lines, political bondings, family interests, and economic necessities that determined who would marry whom. The idea of love as having a place in these arrangements was not even contemplated.

> It was not until the Middle Ages that the word "love" (in the sense in which it is used today) became current.... When the Crusades began in the eleventh century, many of the nobles went off to war, leaving their wives at home. [It was] during this period that the phenomenon of the troubadour, usually a noble who went from castle to castle to entertain, arose. These troubadours sang songs and ballads about "romance" [which idealized passion] to entertain the lady of the castles. [Implied was an unrequited or adulterous love that remained outside of marriage.]...This was the genesis of "romantic" love. Like most human beliefs, attitudes, and ways of behaving, it grew out of the social conditions and requirements of an era, and represented an adjustment to these conditions.[1]

At present, the idea of romantic love is taken very seriously. The seeking of a "soul mate" (one who walks the same path in a complementary fashion) is a primary goal for a great number of people. When a person has the sense that he or she has found this magical other, there is an inclination to join with the other and become as one. The Sufi poet Rumi wrote, "The minute I heard my first love story I started looking for you, not knowing how blind that was. Lovers don't finally meet some-where. They're in each other all along."[2]

When we find this ideal other we experience a reflection of wholeness and unity on an inner level. This is a feeling one wants to hold on to, and thus develops the desire to marry. Love offers this gift of such powerful significance, and the rewards and intricacies of love are legend.

Marriage is one of the most profound passages of life that a person experiences. This is because it includes three significant stages, simultaneously incorporating an ending, a merging, and a beginning. Passage through all of these stages is accomplished as one leaves the child role designated in the family of origin to become partners with another similarly independent adult and establish a family of one's own.

According to anthropologist Arnold van Gennep, a transition ritual like a wedding changes the balance in social relationships. The ritual or ceremony is aimed at allowing the individual to have a "safe journey." Gennep described three stages which must be undergone. The first, he calls separation; next comes a threshold period where one bridges both realities; and finally there is a period of incorporation, where "ordinary" life is resumed but from a new position, status, or situation.[3]

When people physically separate from their families of origin, they will still carry many of the values, behaviors, and traditions developed in those families over the years. Imagine two very different people coming together in a relationship. Certainly there will be many common interests and feelings. The obvious differences can provide opportunities for each partner to grow. But these differences must be understood; and the partners' acceptance of each other "as they are" must underlie the negotiations and compromises that must be made. A successful marriage, then, will be one where both parties are commited to working with and working through differences.

Denis de Rougemont stated this understanding in words that can easily be incorporated into the text of a wedding ceremony:

> To enjoy what has been given one must discover the one essential—a sense of constancy. For to be faithful is to have decided to accept another being for his or her own sake, in his or her own limitations and reality, choosing this being not as an excuse for excited elevation or as an "object of contemplation," but as having a matchless and independent life which requires *active* love.[4]

Wedding

Whether or not one fully understands the symbolism of marriage, the wedding will enact many of the elements of this symbolism as well as the elements of the passage represented. If the ritual is done well, the transformation that results in each person and in the relationship will be eloquently expressed and will bring about an enduring difference. A wedding ceremony is a ritual. Ritual is "a series of symbolic acts focused toward fulfilling a particular intention."[5] For most people, the intention expressed in a wedding is to make public and formalize the love and commitment in the relationship. This is what the part that occurs between the processional and the recessional—the ceremony itself—is about. However, if you look at a ritual as having four separate steps—the first is *planning*, next comes making *preparations*, then the *manifestation* or ceremony itself, and finally the completion or *incorporation* of what has taken place—you can begin to see how the creation of a wedding can become an experience of unfathomed dimensions.

The organization of all these details can be handled by a wedding consultant. He or she can assist with the minutiae of the planning and preparation stages. These can include finding an appropriate site, a printer for the invitations, a florist, a caterer, a band, a jeweler, an officiant, and whatever else might be required. The manifestation stage of the ritual is the job of the officiant. Presiding can be a priest, rabbi, minister, ship's captain, public official, or whatever is acceptable in your state.

The "job description" for this person really depends on your needs. What do you want this person to say, and how, and when? Yes, you can decide what will best represent your specific needs for this momentous occasion. This is where this book becomes a vital instrument in the creation of a memorable wedding.

In the following pages you will not only come to understand the value of creating a personalized ceremony but also learn exactly how to do so. By following the guidelines presented in the succeeding chapters, you will have a simple structure that will take you into and through the process of planning, preparing, expressing, and integrating the marriage ceremony and all that it symbolizes.

CHAPTER ONE

THE NEED FOR A PERSONALIZED WEDDING

WHEN MY PARENTS wed back in 1946, they were a relatively young Jewish couple who had immigrated to this country some years earlier. Both were from Orthodox families that followed the traditional customs. My father's family had a close relationship with a rabbi they knew in Odessa. Eventually they were able to bring the rabbi to this country. Needless to say, he was chosen to perform my parents' wedding. My mother, having a mind of her own, wanted to have her input in the ceremony, too. She found another Orthodox rabbi to assist the officiant as a cantor. Along with his choir, the cantor provided the music for the ceremony.

My parents were married under a *chuppah,* or canopy, said to represent the home. The invocation was read, the betrothal benediction was recited over a glass of wine from which both parties drank, my father placed the ring on my mother's hand and recited in Hebrew, "Thou art consecrated unto me with this ring as my wife, according to the law of Moses and Israel." At the end of the ceremony the glass was wrapped in a cloth and placed beneath my father's foot, where he smashed it. This was to symbolize the destruction of the Temples in Jerusalem, as well as to remind those present that joy and sorrow, creation and destruction are born together.

What was said and what was done were not questioned. This was the way a Jewish wedding was performed. What brought my parents together, how they felt about each other, what they wanted for and from each other in the years to come—none of these things were questioned, and were not addressed. I never could figure out why my parents were together. Perhaps this was because they had never really thought about it themselves.

Nowadays people do think about why they are marrying. In general, times are very different than they were when my parents wed. It is not uncommon to marry later, to have multiple marriages, interracial, interethnic, or interfaith marriages, and even same-sex marriages. In recent decades, women have had the freedom to discover their identity outside of and beyond that of wife and mother. This alone has made different demands upon relationships, changing the traditional notion of marriage.

Even more importantly, from the sixties on people began asking questions and challenging authority and tradition. When long-held practices became outworn, creative adjustments or replacements were often made. Times and information have changed so drastically in so many areas over the past several decades that new words, new beliefs, and new practices have been developed out of necessity.

All the changes our world and our society have seen have impacted the family in profound ways. Marriage used to be a civil and community-supported arrangement designed to insure physical survival of the family. Now single-parent families, broken families, blended families, and other variations are more commonly found than the traditional father-mother-children set-up marriage was sanctioned to protect. Currently, when people marry it is more for emotional and psychological survival than for the survival of the nuclear family unit.

Adapting Tradition to Meet Your Needs

In other words, what marriage symbolizes is not a static concept. Marriage is an evolving idea which continuously unfolds. To the ancients, the wedding that featured the union of a man and a woman was symbolic of the creation of all life. Throughout history, to many people marriage symbolized the conjunction, or myth of unification, of the divine forces. It was also the reconciliation of opposites as seen in the yin-yang symbol. This symbol of complementarity portrays the perfect balance of the two great forces in the universe, each flowing into the other and each containing the seed of the other. In many ways marriage will always represent these things, and yet it must also represent the meanings and needs of the times.

The traditional ceremonies often include such phrases as "man and wife" rather than husband and wife, or man and woman. In the vows the woman pledges to obey while the man promises to worship. *The Alternative Service Book* points out that

> Until comparatively recently the headship of the husband in the family and the subordination of the wife to him has been accepted in Christian society as well as the other societies. Today there are many Christian couples who do not share the view that sexual differences between partners are the basis of fundamental distinction of status as between husband and wife. This point of view does not seek to minimize the differences between male and female but suggests that the relationship of wife to husband is complementary rather than subordinate and believes "that symmetry and not subordination is the mark of a good marriage."[1]

But even an orthodox ceremony can be nicely adapted for those who are attracted to tradition. The following excerpt from the standard Episcopal ceremony is from the Book of Common Prayer, dated 1945.

On the left is the original ceremony and on the right is a modification that still holds much of the tone of the original.

Dearly beloved, we are gathered together here in the sight of God, and in the face of this company, to join this Man and this Woman in holy Matrimony; which is an honourable estate, instituted of God, signifying unto us the mystical union that is betwixt Christ and his Church…therefore [it] is not by any to be entered into unadvisedly or lightly; but reverently, discreetly, advisedly, soberly, and in the fear of God. Into this holy estate these two persons present come now to be joined….

[Request for disclosure of possible impediments to the marriage.]

_____ wilt thou have this Woman to thy wedded wife, to live together after God's ordinance in the holy estate of Matrimony? Wilt thou love her, comfort her, honour, and keep her in sickness and in health; and, forsaking all others, keep thee only unto her, so long as ye both shall live?

I will.

Welcome. Today we have come together to witness and celebrate the joining of this man, _____, and this woman, _____, in marriage. A marriage between a man and a woman is said to symbolize a mystical union. This is something not to be entered into lightly, but carefully, with reverence, and serious consideration. _____ and _____, you two have now come to be joined in this sacred bond.

Do you both come to this marriage freely and of your own choosing?

We do.

_____ will you take this woman as your wedded wife? Will you promise to love her, comfort her, and honor and support her in sickness and in health, being faithful to her in all your days together?

I will.

[Repeated for the partner.]

I _____ take thee _____ to my wedded Wife, to have and to hold from this day forward, for better for worse, for richer for poorer, in sickness and in health, to love and to cherish, till death do us part, according to God's holy ordinance; and thereto I plight thee my troth.

[Repeated for partner.][3]

[Repeated for partner.]

I _____ take you _____ as my partner in marriage, to have and to hold from this day forward, for better and for worse, for richer and for poorer, in sickness and in health, to love and to cherish, through all the days of our lives.

[Repeated for partner.]

There really are no rules regarding the content of the ceremony. This gives you the option to use any previously written material in any way that embraces your needs. Adapting the wedding to be more current can speak to a number of differing requirements. Let's look into some of these categories in more detail.

Second or Third Marriages

When either partner has been previously married, an appropriate ceremony might address not only the different understandings and expectations each person might have of marriage, but also issues of blending families. When each partner has a child or children from prior relationships, their participation in the ceremony can symbolize this blending and the equal importance each partner's children hold. My experience with couples who have children from previous marriages is that they often wish to include their children in the ceremony. This both helps the children feel more established as members of the new family and gives them an opportunity to bless the union by their participation.

One couple with older children had the children participate by doing a smudging at the beginning of the ceremony. Smudging is generally thought of as a Native American ritual, but the use of burning incense or herbs for cleansing is actually common to many traditions. Early in the ceremony I stated, "In many traditions a new beginning is preceded by a cleansing ceremony in which sweet herbs are used to purify the ritual space as well as our own inner space." The children lit some sage and sweet grass in a shell and carried the shell around a circular area that would be used as the ceremonial space. They then passed the shell around each person in attendance, symbolically cleansing and readying everyone for beginning the ritual.

Another couple with a young daughter modified the traditional flower girl role by having the child lead the ceremony. She entered the ritual space strewing potpourri along the path to the altar. There she waited while the betrothed walked together over the petals. When they reached the altar they both embraced her and kissed her, thanking her for the good job she had done, and sent her to sit with a relative.

While children are a vital element of a person's history that must be recognized, another important consideration for couples who have been married before is how to put away the past. Whether one has been married once, twice, three or more times, the new marriage should be approached as if it will be lasting.

A couple in their forties who both had been married in the past wanted to acknowledge that their former relationships and the many things they had each experienced over the years had been steps leading to their coming together. They also wanted to state the many ways they had grown and the lessons they had learned that helped them feel they could now come to the marriage with health, wisdom, stability, and open-mindedness. They asked me to include in their ceremony this statement about marriage:

> Marriage is a daily challenge which must be met with acceptance, confidence, and awe. There is no way to understand how you will change and grow from day to day, no way to prepare for the enigmatic drama of life. In your past marriages, in your relationships with friends and family, and in the many experiences of your lives, you have learned tolerance, flexibility, and patience. You now both feel you have acquired and developed the necessary resources that will enable you to share your lives successfully. You are not afraid to make mistakes or to ask for help; and, most importantly, you do not expect every moment to be as perfect as those you are sharing right now.

Also in the ceremony was the following poem by Adrienne Rich:

> Since we're not young, weeks have to do time
> for years of missing each other. Yet only this odd warp
> in time tells me we're not young.
> Did I ever walk the morning streets at twenty,
> my limbs streaming with a purer joy?
> Did I lean from any window over the city
> listening for the future
> as I listen here with nerves tuned for your ring?
> And you, you move toward me with the same tempo.

Your eyes are everlasting, the green spark
of the blue-eyed grass of early summer,
and green-blue wild cress washed by the spring.
At twenty, yes: we thought we'd live forever.
At forty-five, I want to know even our limits.
I touch you knowing we weren't born tomorrow,
and somehow, each of us will help the other live,
and somewhere, each of us must help the other die.[3]

Same-Sex Marriages

Although not yet recognized as legal by the State, marriages between people of the same sex are not uncommon. Some couples choose to make a commitment equivalent to that in a heterosexual relationship and may choose a ceremony that parallels some of the more traditional ceremonies. Some find that they can use a traditional ceremony more or less in its original form, while for others the only changes required are those that relate to old-fashioned gender roles. The following is an example of one such ceremony:

Greeting

Officiant. Welcome! Thank you for coming to affirm and celebrate this bonding of love between _____ and _____. They both feel that your presence makes this occasion even more special; that the love and support from every one of you in this circle have provided stepping stones to this moment. What you each have given to them as individuals and as a couple has been integral in bringing them to this stage in their relationship. Love and unity with each other on a personal level is what lets us recall and perhaps restore our sense of unity with the Great Spirit.

When people spend years together they grow together in many ways. They grow in understanding, and connection, and security. As individuals they gain more freedom to be themselves as each partner continues to support and affirm the growth and changes of the other. In the years that you two have been together, you have discovered that your relationship has brought you many things: strength, commitment, sharing, challenge, communication, sensitivity, forgiveness, and love.

Officiant reads a quotation from Corinthians.

Wine Ceremony

Officiant. The cup or chalice is an ancient symbol for the feminine, and wine for blood or life, and consanguinity. As you both drink from this cup, may it serve to mark the sharing you experience as women together, as well as the recognition of your spiritual union.

After the wine ceremony came the exchange of vows and rings. Each partner had written very personal vows to the other which were read aloud while the couple held hands. After stating their pledges, they exchanged rings, saying, "I give you this ring as a symbol of my love and commitment."

A friend then sang a song to the couple. At the end everyone joined in and sang the chorus several times. When the singing ended, the couple kissed and everyone applauded.

This joyful celebration by friends and family worked beautifully for this couple. Other couples may wish to speak specifically of the personal and political issues surrounding a same-sex marriage. Such a ceremony might be similar to or entirely different from the one above. Any couple can celebrate their commitment or recognize their spiritual union in a ritual which includes supportive friends and family members. These rites can make a profound difference to the couple, who are making a public proclamation of their feelings despite the difficulties they may face in finding widespread acceptance for their convictions.

Marriage is always a challenge, but when two people are not only different from each other as individuals but also "different" as a couple in the eyes of the world, those challenges may be greater. Working through these issues frequently serves to bring partners even closer together because of the efforts they must make to really understand and accommodate the elements of difference.

Intermarriages

Peoples and cultures in every part of the world have some sort of ritual to represent and honor marriage. The men and women that have come to this country over the years have brought with them the heritage of many traditions holding great beauty and significance. When people of different races, religions, or ethnicities decide to marry, a ceremony that includes something from each partner's background is valuable for a number of reasons. In addition to enhancing the ceremony with elements from a particular tradition, using symbols from each party's heritage helps bring understanding and acceptance of the differences into the ritual and perhaps even into the marriage.

Drawing from Special Traditions

A 1991 article entitled "The Rites that Bind," for example, describes a !Kung wedding in South Africa, [in which] "the parents of the bride and groom each bring a brand from their own family fires, and together start a new fire for the family unit."[4] This custom or an appropriate adaptation can be brought to modern weddings in this country, as can meaningful rituals from many traditions.

A Persian friend told me of his wedding, during which he and his partner were seated before a cloth laden with a variety of items, each with special significance. Eggs and walnuts painted silver symbolized a wish for abundance and prosperity, as did bowls of coins and plates of cheese, vegetables, and bread. Candies represented the sweetness life holds. A clear bowl of water in which candles floated showed the brightness of life and the flame of love. A mirror was placed before the couple to show their images reflected together and held within the perimeter of the frame.

In a Hindu ceremony, *Collier's Encyclopedia* explains, "the bride and groom take seven steps together, symbolic of their common journey through life, and the bridegroom recites traditional mantras to the bride: 'I am the words and you are the melody; I am the melody and you are the words.'"

Any of these customs, or traditions from cultures that are personally meaningful to you, can be adapted for your needs. In the following ceremony, for example, the couple wanted to acknowledge being from different countries as well as an affinity with nature and some of the more pre-Christian traditions.

Entrance

The couple enters from the ocean and comes to the altar, taking their bowls of grains—hers filled with oats to represent her Scottish heritage and his filled with cornmeal to symbolize his American roots. They separate and cast the grains in a circle, coming back together up the center to the altar, where they set down the bowls.

Welcome

Officiant. On this, one of the most important days of your lives, you stand within the wondrous circle of your love; in this oasis of beauty alive with the spirits of nature; and surrounded by the presence of your dearest friends who are here to witness and participate in your marriage, as well as by the thoughts of those who cannot be here and would have greatly loved to share this experience with you. As you stand within this loving circle, may you not only draw from the unity, wholeness, and perfection symbolized by the circle, but also recall the ancient and modern meaning of being within a sacred space.

You two have chosen to have this ceremony as a way to publicly declare and enact your union with each other. You have expressed the wish to acknowledge, articulate, and share what you are experiencing together with everyone here, as they are all people with whom you also share love. This is a time when you can create a magical and unforgettable celebration of love, where you can renew the intensity of your wonder and appreciation of each other, and re-affirm your purpose and intent to yourselves and each other as you bring forth the images of perfection that will guide you in your commitment.

The basis for this commitment that you have made and are continuing is not only love, but friendship, freedom, open-hearted communion and expression, the shared heart, and compatible values and lifestyle. In your union you can continue to be playful as companions and friends as you expand your knowledge of the meaning of relationship. Your marriage can enable and support spiritual growth and discovery for both of you, and expand your capacity for love, intimacy, and joy.

You gave me a beautiful and inspiring list of the intentions you would like to fulfill in your marriage. Recall these words and take them in as affirmations for the future: to unfold the adventure of marriage; to explore the world together; to tell the truth; to love fearlessly; to feel how real and present your union is from moment to moment; to live your dreams; to open fully to brilliant mundanity;

to meet in unconditional love; to be fully awake to who you are; and to be a happy family.

Candle Ceremony

Officiant. The flame of the candle represents not only illumination but also spirit; and fire is often said to symbolize inspiration and aspiration, power and passion. As you each bring these qualities from within yourselves to your union and your family, may you find the flame burning always brightly in your hearts. *The couple lights the central candle, with it the daughter's candle, then those for the other children.*

Water Ceremony

The officiant pours water from the cup to the chalice and holds it. To you, _____, water symbolizes rain, tears, cleansing, and healing. You, _____, find depth and fluidity in water. Generally, water represents feelings, emotions, and that perception of being able to have a sense of what another feels. As you both drink from this chalice, may all the meanings flow together.

Grain Ceremony and Vows

Officiant. From water we move to earth. The element of earth gives us a way to ground or make real and tangible that which was born as an idea or feeling. Grain represents potential and the seed of life. As you make your vows to each other, know that in your marriage you can substantiate your potentials. *Each partner takes a bowl of grain and states the meaning of its contents.* As you state your vows, let your grains blend in the marriage basket. *The bride has written a poem about the marriage basket, and each partner has prepared a list of twelve promises. The bride reads her poem, then the couple take turns reading their vows one by one, sprinkling a handful of grain into the marriage basket with each pledge.*

Closure

Officiant. With the joy and blessing of all present here, we recognize that you are husband and wife.

The couple kiss, then turn, reaching into the basket and grabing handfuls of the blended grains, which they shower over themselves.

As you can see, the beliefs and customs that have meaning for any one individual can be handed down through generations or can be adopted because of natural affinities. Whether you draw from traditions that are part of your heritage or create traditions that resonate with your spirit, discovering what does have meaning for you is what is important. When people of differing backgrounds come together, it is because something of great value is shared. Expressing what the two of you hold common and what in you is different but compatible can make for an outstanding ceremony.

CHAPTER TWO

CREATING A RITUAL

N O MATTER HOW similar to or how different from your partner you are, and no matter how much you both are like or unlike anyone else you know, your wedding should speak specifically to what marriage means to the two of you. Remember, a wedding is a rite of passage. It marks a major life transition. In psychological jargon, a marriage is a stressor, having a moderate impact on one's ability to function in a healthy way.

I spoke with one couple whose ceremony I had performed, a month or so after they returned from their honeymoon. The husband said, "We've been feeling strange since we returned from our trip. Planning the wedding took so much time and thought, there was always something to do." People think of the wedding rite itself as the high point of "getting married," and it is. Still, it is only one stage in the four-stage process I described in the introduction. The ceremony is the stage of manifestation, in which all the planning and preparation culminate. However, the planning and preparation stages are part of the ritual, too, as indicated by the sentiments of the young man above. After the ceremony, and even after the honeymoon, when the post-wedding lack of direction is likely to set in, there is still something to look forward to. Of course you are in the state of "being married," but at this time you also begin the fourth stage of the process, evaluating and incorporating all that has passed.

Once you can break the ritual process into manageable components, you have a better chance to negotiate each of the stages successfully. Understanding how a ritual unfolds can help things run more smoothly. Take a few moments to imagine (or remember) the following scenario: You and your partner are both aware that you feel a deep and abiding love for each other. It is probable that you also feel respect and affection, have some common interests and goals, and share a compatible lifestyle. You both have decided that you wish to be together in an important and most likely exclusive relationship for a long time. Each of you feels committed to your partner and to the relationship. You decide to marry. Now what? What does this mean? Is it just making this declaration to each other, or going through a legal transaction at city hall? For many people there is a desire to make this a public declaration. This is the first step in the ritual process: defining your intention.

The process of creating a ritual begins with finding a specific answer to the question, "Why is this ceremony going to take place?" You will find that in discovering the answer to this primary question you will also be answering many other important questions. Aside from legal purposes, a wedding usually occurs so friends and family can witness, bless, and celebrate the coming together of the lives of two people during a ceremony that consecrates or sanctifies their love. This *raison d'être* appears to be fairly specific, yet the more explicit you become, the more you will be taking care of the first stage of the process—planning.

For example, if you want those invited to your ceremony simply to witness the event, they become an audience, and the planning is done somewhat as for a performance. Or, if your guests are being invited to bless the marriage, the blessing can be passive, implied by their presence, or more active—you can invite some or all of those in attendance to offer blessings in some specific manner. Celebrating, too, can be active or passive. You have a wide spectrum of options here. A celebration can be simply the marking of an event. It can be solemn or festive or some combination thereof. Some couples choose to have a dignified wedding service and save the merriment for the reception. Others prefer that their friends and family participate in the rite with singing, chanting, dancing, or any number of other possibilities.

Planning

The planning stage includes all these considerations and more. We will talk about the specifics of planning your wedding in chapters 3 through 5. For now, we will look more generally at how best to approach this stage of the ritual process. Once you have both come to a clear agreement about why you are having a public ceremony and what you want it to accomplish for yourselves and your guests, you must determine how your needs will best be expressed. Remember, the ceremony is the magic moment, a time to cherish for years to come. Therefore the planning of this important ritual should be undertaken with the care and consciousness it deserves.

As I explained in the introduction, a ritual is a ceremoniously performed series of acts with some implied purpose. Through the symbolic design of these acts, we form a connection with the unconscious as we begin to speak its language. In each of us there is a personal unconscious which holds that which has passed from our individual conscious awareness, and a collective unconscious which holds the common human heritage of possibilities. The ritual process itself is common to all peoples historically and cross-culturally.

So a wedding is much more than a tradition in which a bride in a symbolic white dress and veil carrying a symbolic bouquet of flowers is escorted by her father to a symbolic altar where she is given to the groom and they exchange symbolic rings and vows. The ritual affords the extraordinary opportunity to tap into the archetype of union. On a spiritual level, this is the ultimate attainment. And certainly, for most couples, a wedding is a very spiritual experience. Remember, the traditional ceremony joins "this man and this woman in *holy* matrimony." Webster's *New World Dictionary* defines "holy" as "regarded with or deserving deep respect, awe, reverence, or adoration." It is being fully present with the whole process that brings this moving and magical power to the ceremony itself. The early stages of the ritual process serve as a kind of incubation period during which the couple are prepared for the transition to a new life and its culmination in the marriage itself.

In ancient Greece there was a dream-incubation ritual somewhat like a vision quest that took place at temples of the God Aesclepius. After a long journey to the temple, a fast or restricted diet, sexual abstinence, ritual cleansing and offerings to the Gods, followed by instructions from the priests and a special dream inviting one to enter the dormitory, the seeker would enter the sacred chamber to await the healing dream. Eventually the petitioner was likely to be visited by the great healer Aesclepius, who would provide the sought-after guidance.

> The journey, the purification, the consultation with the priests, and finally the days and nights alone in an inner chamber culminating in a powerful dream, must have greatly affected the state of mind of the supplicant. The result was an *altered state of consciousness,* that is, a radical change and renewal of the life of the ego by means of its contact with an irrational, energizing experience. No deep healing is possible without such an altered state of consciousness, and no one should approach the god for healing unless he is willing to undergo it. Techniques of meditation, prayer, initiation, and incubation are designed to produce experiences that will alter our state of consciousness, and in this way make possible the infusion of new life and energy.[1]

A comparison of the ritual process of the vision quest to that of a wedding is not as remote as you might think. In both rituals the process is very much an encompassing passage from beginning to end. Even a simple ceremony can entail quite a bit of planning. Considering exactly what you want your wedding to include, how you want things to proceed, when and where the event will occur, who will be involved and how, who will be hired and for what, what must be purchased and how it will be paid for are all part of this stage. In addition there has to be agreement between you and your partner on all these decisions. Dealing with these concerns and demands is going to evoke a lot of different feelings within you and between you. These feelings will be heightened as pressures increase and the time of the event grows near. But remember, this is all a journey. Enjoy all of it. Let each concern and development become something that deepens and strengthens your relationship.

Preparation

After you have formulated the creative design for your wedding ceremony, you must prepare physically, mentally, and emotionally. This is the stage where you must do the leg work; and it does require quite a bit of work. Much of this is making contacts. There will be a number of people you must either hire or enlist friendly aid from. Some professionals will be able to recommend others. Or, you might want to use a wedding consultant at this stage. A consultant functions as a general contractor. He or she will have referrals for you for most everything you need.

To date, I have not performed a wedding for anyone who has used the services of a paid consultant. However, this role is frequently assumed by the mother(s) or even father(s) of either partner. Having such assistance can be invaluable, but it is wise to make the important decisions yourselves. For many couples the wedding marks a separation from their families of origin and a statement of their new status as a separate and unique family. Consequently, preparation for the ceremony can bring emotional conflict as one is pulled between two identities—the parents' child and the independent adult. In the long run, it makes for a healthier relationship for the couple if their primary allegiance is to each other. And, although the details of preparation can sometimes be overwhelming, working them out with your partner can also create precious moments of sharing.

One couple found a way to have the best of both worlds. They decided that they wanted a ceremony in which all their friends could have an active part. Everyone joined creatively in a cooperative effort to produce the celebration. Those with special skills donated something that represented their talent, and in some instances this contribution was the wedding gift. A friend who was a musician provided the music, another danced, and still another was responsible for the decorations. Some had relevant businesses or business connections, and from these friends came the flowers and wine. Family and friends read poems and blessings they had found or written. Rather than buying a wedding cake, the couple asked a number of the guests to bake small cakes. Each was a beautiful and unique presentation. The heartfelt involvement and participation of one and all turned the ceremony into a true celebration of love and union.

This wedding was genuinely unique and beautiful, but many couples feel more comfortable, for numerous reasons, following a more standard procedure of preparation. In the past it has been the rule rather than the exception for the parents of the bride to take care of most of the expenses, with the groom's parents handling certain other expenses. For some couples, particularly young heterosexual couples marrying for the first time, this may still be an option. But for older couples, couples marrying for the second or third time, or couples who do not have the blessing of their families, the financial responsibility must be personally assumed. For these couples, including friends or family in a cooperative way can help ease costs and, even more importantly, create a close and loving atmosphere that truly supports the spirit of marriage.

However you decide to assign the tasks and responsibilities, you will find that managing the essentials of the preparation stage clearly segues right into the next stage of manifestation. You might find it helpful to schedule a break for yourselves in the twelve to twenty-four hours before the ceremony. I remember one bride who had a massage and hot tub the morning of her wedding. This served as a valuable transition point for her and one that, in fact, was an integral part of weddings in days gone by. In ancient Greece, for example, the bride

> was expected to take a ritual bath in water that had been carried from a special fountain. In Athens both the bride and groom bathed in water from the spring of Kallachoran to insure the birth of children....During Elizabethan times, it was common for the two main bridesmaids to come to the bride's room the morning of the ceremony to dress her, while the groomsmen would be at his house trimming his hair and beard, and adorning him with flowers and ribbons.[2]

Such acts serve to mark the moment of transition with cleansing or purification, symbolically releasing the concerns of the past so that a new life can be entered into feeling clear and free. The time just before the ceremony is also a time to ground and center. In times of great excitement we get caught up in the frenzy of our experience, so that it's as if the experience is all there is. When you just *stop*...and take a long, slow breath in...and blow it out through your lips with deliberation, you bring your attention back to your self. You can become aware of your body, the feelings in it, the aliveness of it, the here and now. This is the time when you're readying to take that dive into the pool. You adjust your stance, take a deep breath and hold it, close your eyes...one...two...three...jump! And the wedding begins.

Manifestation

Now we are involved in the manifestation of the event. You will want to recognize the ceremony as a dramatic enactment. At the site you have chosen for the ceremony, there will be a specific place where the rite will take place. This area may be designated by ribbons, flowers, an altar or altars, an arrangement of chairs, a tent or canopy, a floor cloth, or whatever is appropriate for your needs. You might think of this area as the stage. The wedding is the presentation.

A presentation can take many forms. Think of a Thanksgiving dinner—either an elaborate dinner you've attended or one you've seen depicted in a movie. The whole day is spent in a bustle of painstaking preparation. Whoever is responsible for the turkey gets up early to begin cleaning, stuffing, and roasting the bird. In a traditional American Thanksgiving, sweet potatoes are baked, cranberry sauce is made, biscuit dough is mixed. In the early afternoon family members adorned for the occasion start arriving, each carrying their special contribution. Someone has made a seven-layer salad, someone else a pumpkin pie. One guest insists that mashed potatoes are vital to the dinner and runs hastily to the store to find the fixings. Somebody has the responsibility for the table. It must be opened to accommodate all the extra extension boards. The good tablecloth is taken from the drawer, as are the matching napkins and the dinnerware, flatware, and glasses. It is decided that there will be candles at each end and a centerpiece of pinecones, fruit, and nuts in a decorative basket. The good smells emanating from the kitchen are beckoning and soon the food must be served. Everyone is called to the table. The candles are lit. The turkey is carried in on a large platter.

But Thanksgiving is more than just a time of feasting, more than just a recognition of the harvest or of the bounty to be shared. It is a time of giving thanks for whatever blessings have been received, and so we join hands and bow our heads. Someone speaks of the good fortune of being able to have the family together, of having made it through another year and surmounted innumerable crises and challenges. Perhaps each person speaks of something he or she is thankful for in life. Time is taken to acknowledge where we've been and where we're going. And many people acknowledge their God at this time, taking the time to feel the connection with Spirit. Then the feasting begins, the abundance of food symbolizing the abundance of love and tradition shared at that table. When the dinner is over everyone is full: full of turkey, full of family, full of belonging.

Now certainly not everyone shares this ideal experience with their family during a holiday, but we can see in the idealized version the reason Thanksgiving has so substantial a place in the hearts of Americans. It symbolizes the unity of the family, sharing with others, and the experience of plenty or abundance. This is the image we all try to reproduce in our own homes, with our own families and friends.

And so it is with a wedding. The ceremony must represent the idealized concept of romantic love. So the setting is made as beautiful and sacred as possible, and the guests take their seats dressed in their finest. The music begins and members of the wedding party come forward and take their places at the altar. Last to enter are the betrothed. They reach the altar and the music stops. There is a moment of silence and the officiant begins to speak. All are in rapt attention, straining to hear every utterance, to catch the subtle expressions on the faces of the couple as they take in the words of the officiant and exchange vows and rings. Then comes the kiss. Friends and family pocket their handkerchiefs and applaud the now-married couple. Everyone has been touched and blessed by love and all that it symbolizes. On the most transpersonal level, this is the ecstasy of love, the state beyond ordinary reality where one is temporarily freed fom the worldly condition of separateness. In other words, the archetype of spiritual union has been evoked.

This of course is the climax, and from here the energy settles. The recessional begins. The couple exit together from the altar in their new married status, and stand where everyone can come to offer congratulations. Toasts are made, and the feasting and celebrating commence. Whether the merrymaking lasts for hours or for days, at some point the couple must leave to consummate the marriage in some fashion. They enter the wedding carriage and are whisked away into the moonlight. One couple, whose wedding I performed, rode off romantically in a horse-drawn carriage under a shower of rose petals.

Incorporation

As romantic as the honeymoon may be, at some point the honeymoon, as they say, is over. Now begins the time when the couple returns to "ordinary" life, ready to integrate their change of status into it. For couples who have been living together for a number of years, this stage may not seem to have the same relevance as it does for those who are actually beginning a life together. However, there are important considerations for any couple. On the public level, there are acknowledgments to be made for gifts and other assistance, and perhaps other details from the ceremony to be resolved. On the legal level, changes may need to be made to bank accounts, credit cards, tax information, and the like. But, the most important work is to be done on an emotional level.

Processing the wedding is a good place to begin. It is likely that many feelings emerged during the ceremony. There is really no way to prepare oneself for the sense of being surrounded by an audience of friends and family who are witnessing an extremely intimate experience, much less for the incredible seriousness of committing to a loving relationship with another person for the rest of one's life. The impact of these feelings, and the sentiments concerning the wedding itself, should be dealt with.

After gaining an understanding of the past, it is valuable to work on the present and the future. Now the two partners begin to acknowledge that they each have a life mate who will offer unconditional love and understanding and fulfill all the other pledges made during the ceremony. This is a time to clarify interpretations and expectations. Remember that the line "And they lived happily ever after" comes from fairy tales. Manifesting the wedding promises in the real world takes patience and work.

A happy marriage does not just develop from being in love. Certainly love is a vital and necessary foundation, but love apart from other feelings and resources will bring you to both the pleasure and the pain of ecstasy. In the words of Kahlil Gibran,

For even as love crowns you so shall he crucify you. Even as he is for your
    growth so is he for your pruning.
Even as he ascends to your height and caresses your tenderest branches
    that quiver in the sun,
So shall he descend to your roots and shake them in their clinging to
    the earth.[3]

It is for this reason that the incorporation stage of the ritual includes a continual processing of needs, feelings, and expectations. I have found that some couples choose to have marriage counseling in the beginning of the marriage as a kind of preventative measure. The most intriguing idea I've come across is having the vows hand-lettered, framed, and hung in a prominent place in the home, then holding a monthly meeting at which the vows are restated and discussed. In this way the essence of the ceremony can live on for years.

CHAPTER THREE

CUSTOMS, THEN AND NOW

I N THE LAST CHAPTER, "Creating a Ritual," I talked in general about the four stages of the ritual process: planning, preparation, manifestation, and incorporation. Now we are going to look at some of the specific customs associated particularly with the manifestation stage—the ceremony itself. In the traditional wedding planning guides, particularly those committed to giving the correct etiquette for every aspect of the wedding, you can find all the particulars for a formal traditional wedding. I am assuming that those of you relying on this book are looking for something less standard or customary, and perhaps even somewhat unorthodox. In this chapter, we will explore many of the traditional customs and offer variations which may better suit your needs.

All over the world beliefs and practices developed among different peoples that symbolized the values and needs appropriate to their conditions and times. As these were handed down from generation to generation they became traditions, sometimes as binding as if they were laws. "Numerous meanings that we experience only as symbols were originally understood as statements about realities."[1] In the ancient traditions of Alchemy, the *hierosgamos*, a sacred marriage between heaven and earth, was a mystical union that insured fertility and abundance of crops.

In many religions and among many peoples marriage is symbolic of the union of divine forces, or of opposites. In this sense it is often connected with the myths of creation. "Myths proclaim...attitudes toward reality. Whether we adhere to them consciously or not, they remain pervasively influential....Myths do not just reflect random attitudes toward reality. Rather, they begin with a perception of reality as a whole and in its light construct an integrated system for understanding all its parts."[2] Myths express themselves in symbolic language.

If we were to consider a modern wedding ceremony as if it were a myth or fairy tale we would not have to stretch our imaginations too far to understand the symbolism. Not long ago I saw an advertisement entitled "Your Perfect Wedding." It began like this: "Engaged? Wouldn't you want the most glorious, wonderful wedding you can dream of? Not just another party, this celebrates the most important steps you'll ever take, and everything should be just right." Many weddings, especially formal ceremonies, actually do attempt to produce a dramatic and romantic dream. Just like that perfect little couple standing on the very top tier of the wedding cake, the groom and particularly (in the traditional version) the bride stand in elegant array on top of the world, enveloped in a vision of love and happiness that will transport them to a new level of lasting bliss.

Historically, however, the symbols most often associated with marriage represent wishes either for fertility or for protection of some sort. Many of the practices in a traditional wedding support the idea of bride as chattel. The standard customs in many weddings are completely outdated, as most originated in the Middle Ages, and the meanings of practices, like the use of groom's men or the giving away of the bride, are derived from traditions that today may actually be offensive. Such customs can still be used, however, if they are adapted to your needs and not merely carried out unconsciously. This is true in all areas of life. X-rays, for example, were once optimistically and ambitiously used. Now that we've discovered that this valuable diagnostic technique is potentially dangerous when overused, the proper precautions can be taken. Similarly, when we understand the meanings of a custom, we can find ways to personalize it—to use it consciously to evoke good feelings without the blind association with inappropriate pasts.

Attendants

An early tradition among predatory and warlike tribes of acquiring a bride was literally to kidnap her. Out of this "charming" custom of marriage by capture came the ensuing practice of having friends stand with the couple. The function of these supporters was to protect against the possible attack of angry relatives attempting to reclaim the bride. Currently, when a couple has attendants stand up at the altar, it is so that friends or family who are very dear to the couple can have an opportunity to actively participate, and also to show their emotional support.

Giving Away the Bride

The custom of bride-purchase developed in later years. From this tradition came the practice of giving away the bride, which was symbolic of the father turning over his daughter to her husband, and that of the bride being carried over the threshold by the groom, to show her reluctance to leave her father's home.

In the processional of the traditional and more formal ceremonies, the groom approaches the altar followed by his best man. Other members of the wedding party follow in designated order. Then the music stops, changes, and everyone stands as the bride makes her entrance on the arm of her father. Together, father and daughter approach the altar where the father turns his daughter over to the groom and walks back to his seat. In other instances, the father stands with his daughter until some point in the ceremony when she is "given" to the groom. As the father releases his daughter, she joins hands with her betrothed.

One couple I married some years back chose to adapt this tradition by having me ask, "How comes this man to this marriage?" to which the attendant witness answered, "Freely, and of his own choosing." Then I asked for the bride, "How comes this woman to this marriage?" whereupon the attendant replied, "Freely, and of her own choosing." In this way the couple was able to acknowledge the transitional stages of the passage into marriage by adapting an old custom to their own needs.

The Bridal Veil

In times when marriages were politically arranged to insure blood lines and family interests, ill will and ill wishes were common treacheries. While friends and neighbors wishing to support the couple and bless them with a secure future might have extended gifts, the offerings of those who were jealous were sometimes of a malevolent sort, and the veil was worn to protect the bride against the evil eye. In addition to providing protection, the veil was used as a sign of purity. In times when a marriage was to provide a beneficial union between families, the bride symbolized the honor of her family. To insure purity of lineage for the family of her husband, it was imperative that she be a virgin. In Victorian times, both the white veil and the long white dress were symbolic representations of the bride's purity. (For the Jews, the white veil or shroud has a different significance. White, as a color of mourning, represents the destruction of the Temples in Jerusalem and the other hardships the Jewish people have endured.)

Like so many of the other elements of the wedding ceremony, wearing a veil is currently only a sentimental gesture or formality. Each symbol in the wedding can be made to express the needs and wants of the individuals participating. For some brides, wearing a veil lends an air of mystery and enchantment. At the moment when the veil is lifted, the bride is revealed as the treasured beloved.

Some brides and even grooms choose to wear garlands instead. This custom was popular with the early Romans as a way of insuring fertility. Today, a flower garland may simply signify beauty, with its circular shape, like that of the wedding rings, representing wholeness and unity.

Rings and Vows

The exchange of rings and vows is a principal symbolic act in almost every wedding. According to *The Woman's Encyclopedia of Myths*, the original Anglican marriage service "came from Anglo-Saxon deeds used to transfer a woman's land to the stewardship of her 'houseman' (husband)." In this ceremony the bridegroom vowed,

"With this ring I thee wed and this gold and silver I give thee and with my body I thee worship, and with all my worldly chattels I thee honor," and the bride responded, "I take thee to my wedded husband, to have and to hold, for fairer for fouler, for better for worse, for richer for poorer, in sickness and in health, to be bonny and buxom in bed and at board till death us depart."[3] With only slight variation, this same speech is still quite commonly used. The ring was also used as a betrothal or engagement pledge in the times of wife-purchase to bind the agreement. The ring was both a "downpayment" on the wife and a symbol of the man's honorable intent.

Most couples still choose to exchange rings as symbols of their vows, and for many, engagement rings are de rigueur. But the ring also shares much of the symbolism of the circle, which signifies wholeness, unity, perfection, and timelessness. So an engagement ring can still symbolize intent—the intent to come together in union; and the wedding band still seals the agreement. For modern couples this agreement is to find completion and fulfillment in lasting love.

The wedding ring functions as both an expressive symbol and a unmistakable signifier that one is joined in love with another. Some couples choose to wear matching bands as a symbol of love. Rings are sometimes specially designed and even inscribed as a way of increasing the symbolic meaning. An inscription within the Sforza marriage ring from the fifteenth century stated, "Two torches in one ring of burning fire. Two wills, two hearts, two passions are bonded in marriage...."[4]

The exchange of rings generally denotes a sealing of the vows. For example, in the service of one young couple who wrote special and intimate vows to each other, I said, "You have chosen to exchange rings as symbols of your vows. To bestow a ring is to transfer power and join individuals as vows are sealed within the strength and protection of the circle. A wedding ring is a symbol that binds each to a new state of union, completeness, and fulfillment. Place these rings on each other's fingers as you state your vows to one another." Each in turn read the promises they had written while placing the ring on the finger of the other.

Another striking use of the ring as a seal of the vows comes from a pagan ceremony. Both rings are placed over a rod or wand which can be plain or decorated. The officiant holds the wand and asks the couple to hold hands and place their hands over the wand and the rings. The officiant then states,

Above you are the stars below you are the stones. As time does pass remember... Like a star should your love be constant. Like a stone should your love be firm. Be close, yet not too close. Possess one another, yet be understanding. Have patience each with the other for storms will come, but they will go quickly. Be free in giving of affection and warmth. Make love often, and be sensuous to one another. Have no fear, and let not the ways or words of the unenlightened give you unease. For the Goddess and the God are with you. Now and always."[5]

The partners are then each asked if they choose to marry. After they answer in the affirmative, the rings are exchanged.

Witnessing

In times when marriages were made to strengthen kinship lines or to improve the social or economic status of the families involved, public witnessing of the ceremony was significant. The complete celebration served as a statement to the community that a marriage had been established. Today, too, something as personal as love shared between two people is made into a public event. Whether the wedding is a civil ceremony or a religious service, witnesses are present.

In a Quaker ceremony, the wedding is held at a monthly Meeting. The guests sit silently and await the arrival of the bride and her bridesmaids, followed by the groom and his groomsmen. The bride and groom join arms and walk to their places between their parents, who are seated on a front bench. The betrothed then rise, clasp right hands, and the groom declares, "In the presence of the Lord and of this assembly, I take thee, _____, to be my wife, promising with divine assistance to be unto thee a loving and faithful husband until death shall separate us." The woman repeats the same pledge to the groom, after which both are seated. A table bearing the marriage certificate is read aloud to all in attendance. Afterwards, all those present sign as witnesses.

Newlyweds undergo a change in their position in the community both socially and legally. Marriage also brings a change in spiritual status. Instituted as a Christian sacrament by Jesus along with baptism, confirmation, the Eucharist, penance, holy orders, and the anointing of the sick, marriage was sanctified in 1493 by the Council of Florence. For the Roman Catholics and the Eastern Orthodox, matrimony is one of the seven channels of grace.

The Sharing of Food and Wine

Christian ceremonies share with Jewish, pagan, and many other traditions a number of the same symbols. Among these are the ritual use of bread and wine. It is quite common for a ceremony to end with feasting. Coming from the word *festival*, feasting is a natural form of celebration. In many cultures an abundant flow of wine is an accustomed feature of the festivities. However, the use of wine and bread within the body of the ritual has a somewhat different significance.

Wine Sharing

Wine symbolizes blood and sacrifice, and therefore represents life-force and vitality. As a form of spirits, wine equates with fire, a masculine principle. Water, on the other hand, is associated with the feminine or the mother, as all life comes from the waters. As such, it also symbolizes potential. Immersion in water is seen as a return to the state of being unborn, both a death and a rebirth through a spiritual cleansing and renewal. Wine and/or water can be shared during a ceremony. They can be used in blessing. Or water can be used for purifying. In any usage, the symbolic significance should be kept in mind. For example, in one ceremony water and wine were sequentially poured into a chalice and I stated, "Water and wine are liquids which represent the moon and the sun and all the complementary opposites in the universe. As you share water from the same cup, you can both drink in the feminine or receptive qualities. And as you both take wine from this cup, you can take in the active or masculine qualities." The remaining liquid was poured onto the earth for the ancestors, who were acknowledged and asked for blessings.

Bread Sharing

The sharing of bread, too, can offer blessing to the wedding couple. Made at the hearth, the center of the home and the earliest altar, bread represents home and family. Perhaps more importantly, it symbolizes the mystery of transformation, as in grain to bread to nurturing or sustenance. For this reason bread is an appropriate symbol of the transitions in status that take place when people marry. There are many ways that bread has been and can be incorporated into a wedding. For example, in one small wedding a bread ceremony followed a wine blessing. After everyone in the circle had shared a cup of wine, the officiant stated, "'Bread symbolizes life; the food of the body and the soul. It is also a symbol of union as having many grains in one substance, and when broken and shared represents shared and united life.'6 Your parents gave you life, and now we are asking them to give you a blessing in your new life together." At this point both sets of parents came forward. Together, the couple held a warm round bread. The parents all placed their hands over their children's and over the bread. Each parent gave a blessing they had previously prepared. The bride and groom then fed a bit of the bread to each other and to their parents. This was a good way to have the parents participate in the ceremony, so that they could symbolically let go of their beloved child with a full and sincere blessing.

The Wedding Cake

The tradition of the wedding cake, too, derives originally from the symbolic use of bread as part of the wedding ceremony. According to *Bride's Book of Etiquette,* "the ancient Romans broke a thin loaf over the bride's head at the end of the ceremony. The wheat from which it was made was a symbol of fertility, and the crumbs were eagerly sought by the guests as good luck tokens." For the English in the Middle Ages, "it was traditional for the bride and groom to kiss over a pile of small cakes. When an enterprising baker decided to mass all these cakes together and cover them with frosting, the modern tiered wedding cake was born." One old custom which can be used creatively today is the baking of trinkets into the cake. "A code in the icing tells where they are, so they can be served to the wedding party: A wishbone for luck, a heart for romance, a ring for the next to marry, a gold or silver coin for good fortune."7

The Kiss

One means of showing the new unity of the couple in marriage is by the joining of the hands of the betrothed at some point in the ceremony. But the symbol that is the final statement on the unity symbolized by the wedding of two people is the kiss.

> A contract of eternal bond of love,
>
> Confirm'd by mutual joinder of your hands,
>
> Attested by the holy close of lips,
>
> Strength'ned by interchangement of your rings,
>
> And all the ceremony of this compact
>
> Seal'd in my function, by my testimony. . . .

Thus recites a priest in Shakespeare's, *Twelfth Night* (V.i. 156–161). In the Middle Ages the kiss, known as the "kiss of peace" and a symbol of trust, was actually given by the priest to the groom, who then passed it to the bride. At some point the kiss, still as a seal, fell solely to the charge of the newlyweds.

The kiss signaled the end of the ceremony. Technically, the service itself was usually publicly performed before the church door. Afterwards the couple would enter the church to hear a wedding mass, and the kiss was the formal end to the complete ceremony. But it certainly was not the end to the ritual.

The Feast

A wedding consisted of three parts: the processional, the ceremony, and the feast. The processional, commencing at the homes of the betrothed, was a lavish spectacle attended by musicians, entertainers, family, and onlookers. After the wedding came the celebration; the extravagance of the festivity was limited only by the funds of the bride's father. Merrymaking could literally go on for days, with feasting on roast stag and game, fish, breads, barrels of beer, and hearty wines. Singing troubadors, musicians, and feverish dancing lent to the gaiety. At some point the newlyweds were reminded of their duty to consummate the marriage and were escorted to their chamber. In many cultures, a sign of achievement as well as proof of the bride's virginity was demanded.

A number of ancient peoples, notably the Greeks and Romans, looked to the bride to produce a male heir. Lineage was of utmost importance and a bride's main function was to bear sons. In patriarchal societies this meant the bride went to live with the family of her new husband, where her sons could carry on the family's name and the family's honor.

Blessing the Union

The vows made during the ceremony are more than just earnest promises of love and faithfulness. When a vow is given it is often made before God, or the Gods. Like an oath, a vow is made in the sight of some energy infinitely greater, and thus is understood to be binding. Historically and cross-culturally, religious and spiritual beliefs and practices are foundational. Most people want their marriage vows to be sanctified and their marriage to be spiritually blessed. People today believe in the power of blessings just as the ancients did. Conversely, there is a tendency to give credence to curses or bad fortune. To ward off the possibility of misfortune and to insure happiness, longevity, prosperity, and fertility, blessings are made both within and after the ceremony.

In traditional Christian ceremonies, benedictions may come directly from the Bible. The following are commonly given: "The Lord bless you and keep you: The Lord make His face to shine upon you and be gracious unto you: The Lord lift up His countenance upon you, and give you peace" (Num. 6:24–26). "What therefore God has joined together, let no man separate" (Matt. 19:6). From the Tao Te Ching comes, "Theirs was the fullness of heaven and earth; the more that they gave to others, the more they had." And from an Apache blessing, "Now you are two people with one shared life before you. Go now into your dwelling place to enter into the days of your lives together. And may your days be good and long upon the earth."

After the ceremony, blessings take the form of good wishes and toasts. Champagne is a widely accepted medium for toasting. Sincere wishes for a long and happy life are often made by the best man or by the fathers of the newlyweds, but anyone can and often does feel the urge to make a heartfelt toast. The final blessing is one everyone is involved in. As the newlyweds are leaving the reception for some romantic destiny, the whole company follows them to their vehicle, showering them with rice, birdseed, or flower petals. As the happy couple begins their first romantic night together in their new identity, they will be enveloped with warm wishes for a fertile start.

Now, with all these ideas in mind, I wish you an abundance of ease and enjoyment as you begin to plan your ceremony!

CHAPTER FOUR

PLANNING YOUR CEREMONY

T HE HEART OF MARRIAGE is commitment. When you and your beloved make a heartfelt pledge to each other, you create a relationship that is truly incomparable.

What makes commitment so important? Each of us is born into a family. Some of us may have felt a deep sense of belonging there, and others may have felt there was no place for them at all. From my professional experience with adolescents and adults, I've learned the greatest complaint people have about their childhoods is feeling they were not recognized and loved for who they were. The longing for this recognition and acceptance can persist into adulthood. Then one day as an adult, you may find someone to love, someone who loves you in return. When this happens for you, you begin to feel that now your needs can be met; now you can be with someone who truly cares for you, respects you, and enjoys you. As your relationship grows and deepens, you come to feel that you want to marry and spend the rest of your life with your beloved. Your identity then changes. You are taking a long step away from your family of origin and your past, and you are beginning your own family. This is a profound transition.

To enable this passage, to permit this shift in identity, you undertake a ritual. As a dramatic event, the wedding ceremony with all its symbolic acts functions as a vehicle through which the transformation occurs. This means you want to create something you can get caught up in, something that will sweep you out of ordinary time into the special and magical time-space of ritual. To do this, every element of the wedding should be carefully considered and woven into a seamless fabric.

Planning the Ceremony

Your planning can begin with all the details that will enhance and support the ceremony. You must select a **site,** and once you have done so you must figure out the floor plan. Where will the ceremony take place? Where will the guests be seated (or stand)? Where will you enter from and exit to? Where will the **music** or musicians be? Are you going to have a particular **theme**? If so, how will you want things arranged? Will there be an **altar** or altars? Will there be **flowers**? You will want to find a florist that can arrange for the decorations and corsages, bouquet, boutonnieres, or wreaths.

To perform the ceremony you will need an **officiant** you feel comfortable with. The officiant can only legalize your marriage by signing a **license** procured from the clerk of the court. A **photographer** or videographer can record the event for you so you can relive the memories. If there will be a reception following the service, you may need to hire a **caterer.** The **cake** will probably come from another source. To take you to and from the site, you might need to look into **transportation**. And what about the guests? You might consider the services of an **engraver** or stationer for the invitations and thank-you notes, and possibly for programs and a guest register. Of primary importance to most couples are the **rings.** You might want to choose rings or have them designed for you. **Apparel** is important, too. There are many options here, depending on how formal or informal you wish to be.

Taking care of all these details will require a good deal of time and energy. You want everything for your wedding to be just right, and with each of these elements properly addressed you can focus directly on the ceremony. When a couple comes to me for their first planning appointment, they are often excited, nervous, scattered, or some combination thereof. In order to calm them down and help them feel comfortable, I use the questions on the following worksheet as a point of focus. Thinking about these questions helps them bring forth latent ideas and feelings. Many of the answers will provide information that will form the ceremony. Perhaps the two of you would like to take some time to go over these questions.

WEDDING PLANNING WORKSHEET

General Considerations

Your Relationship

• How did you meet?

• How long have you been together?

• What made you decide to marry?

• What does marriage mean to you?

Intention of Ceremony

• Why a public ceremony?

• What do you want the ceremony to accomplish?

• Who else will be participating and how?

Specific Considerations

Setting

- Where will the ceremony be held?

- What is the setting like?

- Will there be an altar?

- Where and how will the guests be situated?

- How will you enter and exit?

Traditions

- What, if any, religious or spiritual traditions do you honor?

- Which, if any, did your parents practice?

- Is there anything you wish to use or avoid from these traditions?

- Is there anything from any other tradition that you would be interested in?

- What other questions or issues might come up for you in using your own or other traditions?

Specific Desires

• Do you have any specific ideas, needs, or wishes for the ceremony?

• Would you like to include music? Where? What?

• Would you like to include poetry? Where? What?

• Do you have a form of creative expression that you would like to include?

Sub-ceremonies

• Would you like to use any of the following, and if so, how?

> bells
>
> smudging (burning incense for purification)
>
> candles
>
> casting a circle
>
> flowers
>
> bread
>
> wine
>
> token or ring exchange
>
> your own vows
>
> meditation
>
> chanting
>
> group blessing
>
> others

Once you have thought about all these points you can begin to organize the information into a useful form. The following outline will give an idea of how a ceremony typically unfolds.

CEREMONIAL OUTLINE

Entrance

• Music

> You may have general background music which shifts in some way to mark the commencement of the ceremony.

• Processional

• Positioning

> Once everyone reaches the altar or ceremonial space, where does each participant stand?

The Service

• Welcome

> This is generally done by the officiant (as is most of the ceremony) and addressed to the couple and/or the guests. The couple can also feel free to welcome the guests and thank them for their presence.

• Statement of intention

> You or your officiant can state the purpose of your ceremony—why you are all here.

- Invocation

- General words about marriage and commitment

- Specific words about marriage and commitment

    What do these things mean to you?

- Vows, rings, and other ceremonies

    These can include wine or other liquids used for toasts or blessing; songs; poetry; bread; candles; flowers; etc.

- Closure

- Blessing

- Kiss

- Recessional

To give you an idea of how this all comes together, I'd like to present a complete ceremony, preceded by a "flow schedule" this particular couple had planned for the day.

SAMPLE CEREMONIAL SCHEDULE

9:30 Bride and groom arrive with best man and maid of honor for photographs.

10:00 Balloons and directional signs are put up in the park by _____. Flowers arrive and are arranged by _____. The rest of the family arrives for photos. Designated friends coordinate setting up the altar, guestbook, gift area, corsages, and bouquets. The caterer arrives and begins setting up. The staff of the facility begin to set up the arbor with umbrella tables.

10:15 The cake arrives and is received by _____ . The champagne is delivered by _____ and given to _____ . The musicians and the videographer arrive and begin to set up.

10:30 The parking attendants begin assisting. _____ and _____ take their positions as "greeters" and _____ takes his position as usher. The musicians begin to play. The officiants arrive.

11:10 The officiants approach the altar, light candles, and give a greeting.

11:15 The processional music begins. The groom and the bride's mother enter and approach the altar, followed by the groom's son and the bride's sister, and finally the bride's father and the bride. The music stops and the ceremony begins.

11:40 After the kiss, hugs, and tears, the recessional begins. The wedding party and the officiants return down the aisle and form a reception line on the patio.

11:45 The caterers begin to serve champagne and hors d'oeuvres. The pianist begins to play, and the buffet is set up.

12:00 The music stops.

12:30 The band begins its first set.

1:00 On the band's break, toasts are made. The cake is cut.

2:00 On the band's next break, the bouquet is thrown by the bride, and her garter is thrown by the groom.

3:00 The band announces the last dance.

3:15 The guests gather on the patio, and are given handfuls of birdseed to toss over the departing newlyweds.

3:30 The bride and groom depart in a horse and buggy. Designated family and friends pack up and clean up.

Creating this schedule gave the couple and their families a structure for the ceremony that helped them feel grounded and confident that everything was appropriately attended to. It was also a good way to forestall some of the complications that occur on the day of the wedding when various helpers and workers want direction. Usually someone or another will go off in search of someone else, who may have an idea about who to ask. With this printed schedule made available to everyone who was actively participating, confusion was greatly reduced.

As you can tell, this couple was very organized. They took the same care in planning the ceremony itself. They chose to have two officiants, myself and a male colleague, and all four of us had several meetings at which we wrote and compiled the ceremony. This is what we ended up with.

WEDDING CEREMONY

Greeting

Officiants. Welcome! I'm Zachary. And I'm Sydney.

Zachary. We are here to celebrate outwardly the marriage bond that _____ and _____ have been creating inwardly these past two years. We officiate together to represent the equality of their relationship, as well as the balance of the inner masculine and feminine which each is working to establish within themselves.

Sydney. _____ and _____ thank you for your presence and loving support. Their love and intention have created this marriage. We are here to help celebrate and acknowledge that bonding. We do not marry them, they marry each other.

Processional

Statement

Zachary. _____ and _____, you have asked me to speak about the qualities you consider crucial to the well-being and long life of your union. The first of these is the courage to be vulnerable, to be seen as you are, with each willing to accept each other in this way. The second is responsibility, the daily attention needed to keep a relationship vital. Next is the open communication needed to support honesty. You also wish to honor the qualities of humor and playfulness you both enjoy, which nurture the inner children in yourselves and each other. These things you promise to keep alive in your marriage.

Rilke, in this passage that you have chosen, speaks to the commitment that you make:

> For one human being to love another human being: that is perhaps the most difficult task that has been entrusted to us, the ultimate task, the final test and proof, the work for which all other work is but preparation....[Love] is a high inducement for the individual to ripen, to become something in [herself]... to become world in himself for the sake of another person.... human love...consists in this: that two solitudes protect and border and greet each other.[1]

Roses Ritual

Sydney. The coming together of "two solitudes" is part of the cycle of growth—the creating and re-creating of boundaries. May you, _____ and _____, give gratitude for the old boundaries that defined your unique individuality, even as you create a new joint boundary with the circle of your love. *(Sydney creates a circle with rose petals around the bride and groom.)* May this space allow you to face each other and know intimacy. May your intimacy bring you to unfathomed heights through monogamy. May you find the stability of a joint center where you can welcome change. And most of all, may you receive each other joyfully, with open hearts, into this marriage.

Candle Lighting

Sydney. _____ and _____ feel that this marriage is a spiritual union. To symbolize the presence of the Spirit that has brought them together, _____ and _____ will light this candle, igniting the flame of unconditional love. May it burn bright.

Blessing

Sydney. Join us now in a few moments of silence as we each, in our own way, honor this union with a blessing.

Vows

Zachary. _____ and _____ do not marry to fill a want in themselves. They marry because they want to deepen their commitment to knowing themselves, to growing in relationship, and to living fully in their community.

_____, do you now choose _____ to be your life companion, to share your life openly with her, to speak truthfully and lovingly to her, to accept her fully as she is and delight in who she is becoming; to respect her uniqueness, encourage her fulfillment, and compassionately support her through all the changes of your years together?

Groom: I do. *He requests the ring from the best man, and places it on the bride's finger, saying,* Receive this ring as a symbol of my love.

Sydney. _____, do you now choose _____ to be your life companion, to share your life openly with him, to speak truthfully and lovingly to him, to accept him fully as he is and delight in who he is becoming; to respect his uniqueness, encourage his fulfillment, and compassionately support him through all the changes of your years together?

Bride: I do. *She requests the ring from the maid of honor, and places it on the groom's finger, saying,* Receive this ring as a symbol of my love.

Proclamation

Zachary. _____ and _____, I now, joyfully, proclaim to your family and friends that you are married!

Kisses and Hugs

Other Planning

In legal terms, a marriage is a contract between two people. The Reader's Digest book *You and the Law* explains that

> In the eyes of the law marriage is a contract whereby a man and a woman agree to enter into a union for life for their mutual benefit, to provide each other with companionship, sexual gratification and economic help

and to procreate and raise children. The fact that none of these considerations may be mentioned at the time of marriage doesn't make them any
the less binding. They are inherent in the marital contract. Many of them
result from customs and religious doctrines that are almost 2,000 years
old and have been incorporated into present-day laws by both our legisla-
tures and our courts.[2]

In planning your wedding, you will need not only to plan the ceremony itself, but also
to take care of the legal requirements, so that your marriage will be legally valid.

Legalizing Your Marriage

In almost all states you can legally obtain a marriage license if you are at least eighteen years old. Someone under eighteen who has written consent by his or her par-
ent(s) or guardian(s) filed with the clerk issuing the license and an order of the
Superior Court granting permission may consent to and consummate a marriage.
The court will usually require the parties to have premarital counseling that covers
the social, economic, and personal responsibilities of marriage. The licenses are
issued by the county clerk.

In California the fee is currently $60 for a regular license and $70 for a confidential license. For a regular license, both of you must get the results of a blood
test, which can be done by a private physician, the health department, or a family
planning clinic; it must include tests for venereal disease and for rubella (German
measles). The blood test is good for up to thirty days. It can be used anywhere in
the state. Out-of-state blood tests can be used if they meet California requirements. Both parties must bring the results of the test along with a birth certificate
or other I.D. showing date of birth to the clerk. The license will be issued while
you wait and is good for ninety days after the issuance date. This license must be
signed by the officiant and one witness at the time of the ceremony, then mailed
back to the court house by the officiant within four days. In states other than
California, the license may be issued immediately or you may have to wait up to
seven days, depending on the laws of the state. The license is usually valid for from
one to three months, although most states allow you to marry immediately.

In California the blood test for venereal disease and rubella can be avoided if you opt for a confidential license. For this type of license, the couple must have been living together for at least ninety days prior to obtaining the license. A witness is not necessary with a confidential license.

This information is given on the back of a California License and Certificate of Marriage:

> Section 4205 of Civil Code states: "Marriage may be solemnized by any judge or retired judge, commissioner or retired commissioner, or assistant commissioner of a court of record or justice court in this state or by any priest, minister, or rabbi of any religious denomination, of the age of 18 years or over or by a person authorized to do so under Section 4205.1. A marriage may also be solemnized by a judge who has resigned from office."
>
> The License and authorization to marry must be used only within the state of California. . . . The completed License and Certificate of Marriage must be registered within four days after the marriage ceremony, by the person performing the ceremony, with the local registrar of marriages (county recorder of the county where license was issued).
>
> The principal purpose for this record is: 1. To establish a permanent record that is legally recognized as prima facie evidence of the facts stated therein for each marriage occurring in the State of California.

There will be some variation in legal requirements from state to state. For example, rules vary about who can solemnize the marriage. In most states this can be done by a member of the clergy—generally a minister, priest, or rabbi—or by certain judicial officials; in some states it can also be done by other specified public officials. You can call your local county courthouse to find out what specific legal requirements are applicable in your area. Technically all you need to be legally married are the license, an officiant, and the desire to be married to each other.

Fourteen states recognize common law marriage. The state gives legal marriage status to a man and woman who have declared themselves husband and wife and have been living together as such. Some states that do not recognize common law marriages will accept the legality of a common law marriage from another state.

Even if you have a common law marriage, your marriage can be made more meaningful with a wedding ritual. Every couple has ideas, values, and needs that express the special qualities of their relationship. Naming these things and enacting them can bring power to the relationship and so to the marriage.

CHAPTER FIVE

DETAILS, DETAILS

I F YOU'VE ALREADY answered the questions in Chapter 4, read the ceremonial outline, discussed ideas with your mate, and are still feeling confused, you've come to the right place. This chapter is going to be the equivalent of a brainstorming session. So get ready to consider creative options. You may find it helpful to have a copy of the outline and your responses to the questionnaire available along with some notepaper so we can do a step-by-step session. Use the following examples to draw from or simply allow them to be catalysts for your own imagination. Remember, you can add or delete anything to make your ceremony express your specific needs.

Setting

I've performed weddings indoors and outdoors; in halls, mansions, private homes, hotels, clubs, and gardens; at parks and other open spaces like the beach or the mountains; and even on a sailboat. Outdoor ceremonies have taken place under trees, tents, canopies, arches, and tepees. We have walked down paths, down stairs, under arches, around circles, and down aisles; and have done so individually, in pairs, and in groups. We have stood apart from the guests, in front of them, and within the circle of the group. Guests have sat and stood, both free-form and in designated areas. Sites can offer a tremendous variety of options. People choose particular settings for many different reasons. The site can determine the kind of ceremony and reception you can have, so it's best to consider special needs before seeking a location.

Some places have specific regulations regarding smoking, the dispensing of alcohol, hours available, the number of guests allowed, and whether food can be served, music played, candles burned, or birdseed thrown. Some places do not have wheelchair access. Some do not have a dressing room. Certain facilities supply or arrange for services like catering and cleanup, and you do not have the option of selecting your own providers. Being aware of your specific requirements in advance can make it easier to insure that you will not have to make significant compromises later.

Summer seems to be the most popular season to hold the ceremony. Many couples choose to have an outdoor ritual in the summer, spring, or fall. Even if you have chosen a date in mid-July, it is best not to assume that the weather will be sunny. Facilities that have an indoor/outdoor option are safest, and you should always have a contingency plan if you are planning an outdoor wedding.

Choose the site according to what feels right to you, but be reasonable. A full-moon ceremony at the beach might be a viable choice if the wedding party will include only a few close friends and an open-minded officiant, but it probably isn't realistic if you want a large or formal wedding with many guests.

Occasionally you can find sites through the Chamber of Commerce. The Yellow Pages will have some listings under headings such as halls, hotels, bed and breakfasts, and park districts. In some locales a thoughtful individual may have done the research and compiled a useful handbook. For example, *Here Comes the Guide*, by Lynn Broadwell, is a worthwhile directory of sites in the San Francisco Bay Area.

When you have chosen and arranged for the use of your site, you may want to take some photographs of the spot and draw up a floor plan. Then you can determine where the guests will be before the ceremony, how they will enter the ceremonial space, and where they will sit or stand during the ritual. If you are having an altar or altars, you can decide where they will be placed. If there is not an aisle or some other entry space, you can cordon one off with flowers, ribbons, or what have you. You, your officiant, and your wedding party (if you are having attendants) will need a specific way to enter and exit, and a special place to stand.

Music

Next, you need to think about the most appropriate way to signal the commencement of the ceremony. This is generally done with music. Think about it. Of the five senses, only sight and sound can effectively mark off the special time and space of the ceremony. If, by chance, there is a way to dramatically change the lighting to designate the beginning of the service, you might want to consider using that to create something really innovative. A while back, I performed a wedding for a couple in their home. I rang bells to get the guests' attention, and invited them to enter the ceremonial space. It was evening and the room was dimly lit. Glowing candles were placed all around. When the company were all standing silently in their places, I started the taped music and turned off the lights. From the dark hallway, through the door decorated with vines and flowers, came the loving couple illuminated by the candles they each carried. They glided up to the altar, lit the marriage candle with their individual candles, and stood before me. The music ended, the lights brightened, and the ceremony began.

Using candlelight in this way was an expressive way to shift the tone and the timing, but most surroundings will not permit lighting to be used effectively. Sound or music can be used successfully in almost any setting. You can have a band, a choir, a soloist, live or taped music. Bells can be rung, chimes chimed, or a long stretch of silence can provide a striking absence of sound.

A wedding I performed some years back took place down in the meadow area of a large state park. Everything had been set up earlier in the day. The guests had arrived and were all talking and waiting for the ceremony to begin. The couple, myself, and a solo saxophonist waited at the top of the hill. At the designated moment, the musician began to play. His haunting notes echoed throughout the valley. He started down the hill and we followed. Still playing, he came to a halt at the edge of the group while we continued through the crowd to the altar. We turned to face the audience and the music ceased.

Along similar lines was a ceremony in which the groom stood at the altar and signaled a musician to begin playing. As the bride came down the path the groom (a professional singer) began to sing "Come Rain or Come Shine." In another ceremony, taped music was used. An elected friend directed everyone to their seats. I stepped up to the altar and waited. Another friend turned on the tape recorder. The chosen music had pauses every few bars. At the first pause, the groom and his best man began down the hallway, at the next the bride and her maid of honor started off. Each came to their proper place at the altar. The volume was lowered and the ceremony began.

One young couple called their ceremony a handfasting. It took place outdoors in a large space, open but private. Altars were set up in each of the four directions. When it was time to start, someone began to play some lovely and lively music on the flute. I caught the hand of the bride, who took the hand of the groom, who grasped the hand of a friend. A chain was formed and we began dancing and skipping around to encircle the altars. As the circle closed, the three of us broke free and went to stand before the northern altar. The flute-playing stopped and the flautist joined the circle.

Then there was the wedding where the guests, almost all musicians, had brought their instruments. Although the ceremony itself had no more than the normal share of musical interludes, at the end of the rite when the newlyweds were exchanging the ritual kiss, a cacophony of sound burst forth from the audience. This semblance of music became the accompaniment to the precessional and a bout of dancing.

Processional

In a traditional wedding, bridesmaids and groomsmen often have semi-active roles in the ceremony. Their parts consist in forming the processional party and then standing at the altar with the bride and groom. In an unusual variation, one couple chose to have their attendants actively participate in the processional by representing the four elements of earth, water, air, and fire. Four poles were symbolically decorated. For the feminine, indrawing elements of earth and water two poles were covered, one brown and one green. For the opposing masculine, outgoing elements of air and fire, poles of blue and red were made. A woman attendant stood at one side of the entryway holding a bowl of smoking incense to represent air and fire.

Positioned across from her was a man with a bowl of saltwater symbolizing earth and water. Slightly further down the path stood another couple. The man held two crossed poles, representing the opposites of fire and water, and the woman held the air and earth poles. The poles formed an arch over the path. As the bride and groom began the processional they passed between the first couple, where they experienced a ritual cleansing. Then they walked beneath the arch to the altar. Thereupon the first couple set down their bowls and each received a pole from the second couple. All four stepped up to the altar and with the poles formed a rooflike structure over the bride and groom, which they held for the course of the ceremony.

Few couples that I have married have wanted large processionals. Those that did wanted all members of their families to participate, or special family members along with special friends. Some even chose to have the officiant as part of the processional. There were couples who preferred to enter together, arm in arm or holding hands; and there were others who favored approaching the altar in sequence. Etiquette books offer the proper prescribed fashion for making an entrance, and couples have asked me if it was important to follow a particular procedure. I always answer, "It is important to do what feels right to you."

Anyone or everyone can be involved in formally entering the ceremonial space. If you are having a large number of guests, it will be easier if they are led to the area in which they will be standing or seated. If you are going to have children at your wedding, it may be a good idea to give them a job to do. While adults can wait in relative silence for the entrance, many a solemn moment has been transformed into a comedic situation by the loudly voiced question of a young child. The processional is a good time for children to participate. I recall one ceremony where a child willingly led me down the aisle and deposited me at the altar. Children who are not too young can carry candles. Small children can strew potpourri, or ring bells. It is generally best to allow them to return to sit with an adult when their part has been fulfilled.

Positioning

Altars are meaningful additions to any ritual, and I will talk about them more in the following chapter. If you are planning to have a single altar, it is likely that the two of you and your officiant will stand before it. You may want to have an altar even if your site has a distinctive spot that seems ideal for the ceremony. On simply a practical level, an altar will provide a place to set the objects that will be used in the ceremony. Your chosen site may have a fireplace and the mantel can then be used as an altar. A burning fire makes a striking backdrop.

Some settings have platforms or balconies that appear perfect for the service. A landing on a wide stairway may be an attractive place for the rite. In an outdoor wedding there may be a deck or a special grove of trees or a spot in front of a garden. If there is no particularly appropriate spot, you can create one with flowers, candles, or some other form of decoration.

When you reach the ceremonial spot, you will probably face either your officiant or each other. Since it is the officiant who does most of the speaking, it is best if he or she faces the guests. I've found a triangular positioning with the officiant at the apex to be the most practical. Attendants can stand slightly apart on either side, or in a kind of arc. Most couples are somewhat nervous during the ceremony. Holding hands and looking at each other, or at the officiant, seems to have a grounding effect.

The Service

Welcome

Occasionally a couple will want to face their guests and thank them for coming to share this important time with them. It is more common for the officiant to do the greeting and the welcome. I am going to present a number of options and perhaps one of them will feel right for you.

Officiant (to the company). Welcome. Thank you for coming to witness and bless the marriage of _____ and _____ .

Officiant (to the guests). Good morning. *(To the couple)* _____ and _____, today you are surrounded by your friends and family who are here to share this experience with you.

Officiant (to the couple). On this, one of the most important days of your lives, you stand before this group of loving friends and family, who are here to participate in and celebrate your wedding.

Officiant (to the soloist). Thank you for the beautiful introduction; and thank you, _____ and _____, for standing with _____ and _____ on this special day.

Bride and groom (to the company). We would like to thank you all for coming here today. This is a very special time for us and we are very happy that you can be with us to offer your support and share in our joy.

You can actually say anything you choose at the beginning of the service. Some couples elect to make a statement about why they have chosen each other. If they are including symbols and practices that are not known to the guests, they may use the opening to talk about these things. Two women explained to their friends and families what led them to the decision to have a formal marriage. They then expressed their appreciation for the loving support they felt from the group.

It is fitting to express appreciation to the company. A wedding is a time of sharing love, and acknowledging the love for friends and family only adds to the depth of the ritual. Some couples wish not only to recognize those present, but to mention those who could not attend the ceremony. These might be friends or relatives in another territory, or loved ones who are ill or have passed on. A wedding is a time when deep feelings are evoked, and it is one of the few times when people feel comfortable being with those feelings. Love, whether felt for your betrothed, your friends, family, your work, the world, ideas, or God, is really the same thing. The wedding ritual creates an context in which the feeling of love in all its manifestations is made available.

Love as Eros is the connecting principle of the universe, the principle of relatedness. Eros is expressed as a drive towards joining. With your ceremony you not only publicly declare your love for each other, but come to experience the caring affection and love of those you have chosen to share the event with you.

Statement of Intention

In stating your intention, you are naming the purpose for the event. Naming something gives it power. It is the first step in the process of manifestation. Your statement of intention might be something like this one, from Khoren Arisian's *The New Wedding*: "Friends, we are gathered here at this hour to witness and to celebrate the coming together of two separate lives. We have come to join this man, _____, and this woman, _____, in marriage, to be with them and rejoice with them in the making of this important commitment."[1] Such a statement lays the foundation for the rest of the ceremony. When the ritual has been completed, everyone present will feel that the couple at the altar has been joined in holy matrimony.

Invocation

An invocation is a prayer or request that the marriage be spiritually blessed. In supplicating the greater forces the marriage rite is made an earthly reflection of the *hierosgamos* or sacred marriage. During the invocation you can call upon the Heavenly Father, the Great Mother, all the Gods and Goddesses, or whatever name for Spirit reflects your beliefs. It is not mandatory that you use an invocation in your ceremony, but if you do it will give the ceremony a more spiritual tone.

A couple whose ceremony followed shamanistic lines used the following piece by William Butler Yeats in their invocation:

Once every people in the world believed that trees were divine, and could take a human or grotesque shape and dance among the shadows; and that deer, and ravens and foxes, and wolves and bears, and clouds and pools, almost all things under the sun and moon, and the sun and moon, were not less divine and changeable. They saw in the rainbow the still bent bow of a god thrown down in his negligence; they heard in the thunder the sound of his beaten water-jar, or the tumult of his chariot wheels; and when a sudden flight of wild ducks, or of crows, passed over their heads, they thought they were gazing at the dead hastening to their rest; while they dreamed of so great a mystery in little things that they believed the waving of a hand, or of a sacred bough, enough to trouble far-off hearts, or hood the moon with darkness.[2]

They continued the invocation by saying, "Our ancestors, all our relations, our friends, our families, the Great Spirit in all things; celebrate with us the bonding of hearts and souls and the beauty of love. Help us see and know the divine presence in all that is, and keep that truth alive for us today and through all our years together."

An invocation can be a simple prayer or a brief acknowledgment of the presence of Spirit. You can insert a religious prayer even if the rest of your ceremony follows an entirely different path.

General Words about Marriage and Commitment

At this point in the ritual it is a good idea to include some words about marriage and commitment in general. You may want to choose quotations or poetry that express your feelings about love and marriage. This is a good place for the officiant, as one who may have performed many ceremonies, to speak of what marriage is about. Because marriage is an encompassing commitment, one based upon trust, acceptance, and forgiveness, as much as on love and happiness, all of these elements can be discussed in their interactive form. For example:

Marriage creates the security for two people to fully open themselves to each other. Within the safety of this commitment comes the opportunity to accept another person as a complete being who experiences both hopes and fears, satisfaction and suffering. Marriage provides a relationship in which you can have and be a lover, an ally, and a partner. And it is only through this commitment that you can discover true intimacy—in which hidden and protected parts of yourselves are permitted to come forth, find acceptance, and help you become whole. The strength this brings enables each of you to open more readily to the world, beginning an unending cycle of reciprocity.

Specific Words about Marriage and Commitment

It is easy to segue from general to specific. After a general statement about love, marriage, and commitment, you or your officiant can speak of what each of these things means to you personally. This is a good time to relate what brought the two of you together, why you chose to marry, and what you hope your marriage will be.

Everyone has a different notion about the meaning of marriage, based on information from a combination of disparate sources. We mix together complex feelings about what we saw in our families with idealized, romantic ideas of love and marriage from songs and stories. Each individual's unique qualities and needs will color all that information in a way that is generally beyond conscious access. Talking with your partner up front about marriage to discover each of your specific requirements, expectations, and flexibilities will help to lay a foundation for a long-lasting and fulfilling relationship.

When you have this talk you may recognize that the two of you will also need to continuously reevaluate these issues as you and your marriage develop. A summarized version of all this can be stated in your ceremony. If you come to realize that certain things about love, relationship, and commitment that are very important to you, you can include them in your vows.

Vows

Some people choose to say things in their vows that are really quite personal. Each partner may write their deepest feelings for the other and reveal these thoughtful sentiments as part of the vows. When vows are written by the couple, either individually or together, they contain tender, heartfelt expressions of affection. You can each say something different and special to each other, or you can both create something to be repeated by each of you. Vows of this nature can be simple and at the same time complete, as in the following example:

I promise to love you,

To remain honest and faithful to you,

To be available for you when you are in pain or grief,

And when you are filled with happiness.

I promise to challenge you always,

To support and nurture you

And to be receptive to the gift of your love.

I love you with all my heart,

And I will love you for the rest of my life.[3]

Another option is to have the officiant state something that you repeat. This choice is good for those of you who are not enthusiastic about public speaking. If this feeling is coupled with nervousness, you may want to opt for just saying "I do," "I will," or "Yes," in response to a question the officiant poses. This can be a question as simple as "Do you take this woman to be your wife?" or it can describe your pledge more specifically: "Do you choose this man as your husband; and do you promise to love and respect him as an individual, nurturing his growth and encouraging his fulfillment through all the changes of your lives together?"

Rings

Many couples choose to exchange rings at this point in the ceremony. The vow can simply accompany the placing of the ring on your partner's finger. A vow of this nature would be, "With this ring I wed you and pledge my faithful love." Some couples do not exchange rings as symbols of their vows, but choose other tokens instead. A woman who had been married several times before wanted to express that this marriage would be a final and lasting commitment; she carried a bouquet consisting of dozens of purple tulips surrounding a single lavender rose. While giving her partner the rose she stated simply, "This rose is a symbol of my everlasting love for you." I have seen couples exchange tangible items like engraved bracelets or other types of jewelry. A few couples have exchanged flowers, and some have exchanged creative gifts or even the reading of poetry. If you do wish to exchange rings, they can be held by a trusted friend or family member, or the rings can have a special place on the altar. I recently heard of a couple who had their treasured dog take the role of ring bearer.

Sub-ceremonies

An exchange of rings or other tokens is a kind of small ceremony within the context of the larger ritual. There are numerous other sub-ceremonies that can be included, such as special blessings, toasts, songs, poetry readings, the lighting of candles, chanting, or what have you. A local woman shared with me a charming flower ceremony she and her partner had created for their wedding. They researched the meanings associated with different flowers and chose five that they liked. Then they selected five close friends to participate in the ceremony. Each person was told the meaning of a certain flower. At a specified time in the ritual, the friends came up to the altar one by one. As they each placed their flowers into a vase which symbolized the marriage, they offered a blessing that included the meaning of the flower: "May this ivy, which represents fidelity, help you always remain true to each other." "These lilies of the valley symbolize the return of happiness. May happiness always follow on the heels of any difficulty." "The bluebell is for constancy. May you find constancy and security with each other in your days together." "Honeysuckle is associated with a sweet disposition. May the honeysuckle help you remain free from bitterness in trying times." "The rose has always been associated with true love. May your love for each other be as glorious as the unfolding rose."

When all the symbolic acts that speak to all of your requirements for a wedding have been performed, you are married!

Closure

Many couples like to have the officiant make a statement announcing their new status. Other couples prefer to be introduced to the guests in their new status. This can signal the end of the ceremony, or you can have the officiant or someone else give a blessing at this point.

Blessing

I prefer to say something that comes from an Apache blessing you will find in complete form in the chapter on quotations: "And may your days together be good and long upon the earth." You may choose to have something of a more religious nature, or you may simply choose to have someone make a toast after the ceremony.

Kiss

I think you can figure this one out yourselves.

Recessional

The kiss is the climax of the ceremony. All of the energy and tension that have been building throughout the rite are released at this point. Everyone is exuberant and proud. The guests have just gone through the whole ritual with you. They are filled with joyous feelings that need to be expressed. At some weddings everyone bursts into applause during the kiss. Some couples choose to hand out small bundles of potpourri at the very beginning of the ceremony. During the kiss, the guests shower the newlyweds with the scented flowers. The guests may continue sprinkling the potpourri over the wedding party as they leave the altar. You may also choose to have music start up at this time.

The recessional can be a reverse of the processional. If it is just the two of you at the altar, you have the option of going to each of your guests at this time (if you have less than twenty people); if you have a larger wedding party, or many guests, you can form a receiving line. It is difficult to avoid having people want to come up to you offering their congratulations. If you choose to avoid this, though, it is possible. One way is to make an announcement as soon as the ceremony ends, and say that everyone should meet you at a particular spot, where so-and-so will be making a toast.

I hope this is beginning to come together for you. In the next chapter we will get even more specific as we look more closely at some of the individual elements in the outline we've just completed.

CHAPTER SIX

SPECIAL TOUCHES

ETTING MARRIED is big business. Just look in any bridal magazine. Ads and articles describing numerous "must haves" and "must dos" for that "special," "unique," "elegant," "glamorous," "romantic," "perfect" event, or portion of the event, are the primary focus. As with any advertising, the purpose is to sell products and services. You probably do want a wedding that can be described by all these adjectives. If so, you certainly deserve to have it. But it's really the people involved that make the wedding. Everything else is "just icing."

One of the best ways to discover how to create an uncommon ceremony is to look at yourselves, as individuals and as a couple. What is special about each of you and about both of you? Of all the people in the world, why did you two choose each other? Really think about this for a moment. People in relationships have a tendency to focus more on their similarities, and what makes them fit together. Many people attempt to ignore or downplay the differences between themselves and their partners for a variety of reasons. Yet your differences contribute to what makes you unique.

Some of the things that define you can be used in developing the touches that will make your ceremony personal and distinctive. Exploring the following questions may give you some ideas:

- What **religion** are you or were you raised? There may be certain traditions you would like to include, such as kneeling at the altar for a blessing or breaking the wine glass underfoot.

- What **spiritual practices** do you honor? Perhaps a meditation or blessing would contribute to your ceremony.

- Does the kind of **work** you do offer up any possibilities? Do you write poetry, make art, or dance? Can you design your attire?

- What about **hobbies**? If you like to read, for example, you can read an excerpt from something.

- Do you have a particular outlet for **creative expressions**? Perhaps you could make a ceremonial object or write a song to be played.

- Do either of you have **children**? How can they join in?

- Will there be guests who are handicapped or have **special needs**? You might want to arrange for someone to sign the ceremony, or whatever is appropriate.

- Are you part of any **community** or organization? Can you include something relevant to that association?

- Do you have **loved ones** who will not be able to attend? How can you acknowledge them and their absence?

- Are there specific **goals** you have for yourselves in your marriage? Try to think of ways you can symbolically represent them in the ceremony.

Symbols

You could say that all the acts in the ceremony are symbolic. Using symbols in an innovative fashion or using personal symbols can help make your ceremony special.

The symbol is the most basic element of a ritual. Deciding which symbols you want to incorporate into your ceremony, where you will find these things, and how you will use them is quite important. The more attention you give to each symbolic item or act, the more that representation can become a thing of power.

For example, one couple in which each partner was multiracial and multiethnic chose to use blending as a theme. Silk banners were made, two for each of the colors of the rainbow—red, orange, yellow, green, blue, indigo, and violet. The banners were attached to short poles which were held by friends standing on either side of the path used for the processional. When the couple reached the altar, the friends followed in pairs, planting their poles in special holders set around the altar. During the ceremony each of these attendants read or sang a piece on love, marriage, friendship, or community that had its roots in a particular culture. The reception was a potluck, and here again, everyone brought a dish that reflected their extraction.

You may each have things in your life that symbolize something important to you. Symbols have a universal as well as a personal set of meanings. To remind you of some of the symbols you can incorporate in your ceremony, here is a condensed list of the symbols discussed in more detail in Chapter 3.

Symbol Guide

Circle: Wholeness, continuity, safety, perfection

Ring: Eternity, joining, completeness, and fulfillment

Wine: Vitality, life, love, and consanguinity

Water: Purification, fertility, the source of life

Bread: Spiritual nourishment, the food of life, substance

Cake: Sharing, the harvest, abundance

Flowers: Fertility, beauty, unfolding, growth

Incense: Purification, prayers rising to heaven, an offering to the Gods or Spirit

Candles: Illumination, something being made conscious, divine light, inspiration

Bells: A summons; purity, harmony; a charm against misfortune

Music: Harmony and rhythm, happiness, expression of feeling

Threshold: Transition or passage from one place or condition to another

Altars: "The divine presence; the sacrifice; reunion with the deity by means of sacrifice.... The steps up to the altar are ritual ascent."[1]

Precious and semiprecious stones, which many couples choose to inset into their rings, also have symbolic connotations. Diamonds are associated with constancy and strength, the ruby with passion and beauty, the topaz with faithfulness and love, the sapphire with truth, the pearl with purity, the onyx with sincerity and conjugal happiness, the opal with fidelity, the garnet with devotion, and the amethyst with humility.[2]

Altars

Altars deserve some special attention. In an article entitled "Altars of Our Lives," Carol Fuller quotes a couple who made what she calls a "subterranean wedding path altar":

> 'For our wedding we planted charm packets underneath the bridal path, representing fate, prosperity, fertility, happiness and love. Each charm contained a leaf from a succulent plant that my parents stole from Golden Gate Park over 20 years ago. We buried the charms at 3 o'clock in the afternoon (the time we were to be married) a week and a half before the wedding. We did it alone. No one saw us.' A partial list of the contents: marigolds, red roses, gardenias and sweet peas (favorite flowers of the bride's mother and aunt), representing fate; old coins, representing prosperity; cowrie shells and 10-cent babies, representing fertility; metallic glitter and flowers from the bride and groom's garden, representing happiness; turtle charms, pet bird feathers and coffee beans, representing love.[3]

An underground altar is a radically different expression of something that is derived from a word meaning high or altitude. Nevertheless, it could be said that these offerings were made to the maternal principle and the idea of things made manifest as represented by the symbol of earth. Using the four elements earth, water, air, and fire in relationship to altars is quite customary in ceremonies that have a nature orientation. A meditative quality is fostered when time is taken to name and discuss the elements and the corresponding directions. This brings a sense of balance to the ritual and more of a sense of spirit to the ceremony. The four elements are usually used with directional altars, but even a single altar can include the recognition of the elemental symbols.

I am most familiar with the tradition that places air in the east, earth in the north, water in the west, and fire in the south. This can be done with a single altar placed in front of the guests, or with a series of altars which can be placed in a number of different ways.

Single Altars

When there is a single or main altar it serves as a marker for where the ritual is to occur as well as a practical addition to the ceremony. The officiant can stand behind the altar with the wedding party before it, or the altar can be situated somewhat behind or before the wedding party—whichever is most appropriate to the setting and the requirements of your ceremony. This main altar can simply be used to hold the items to be used in the ritual. It can also hold decorative items like flowers, or ritual items that are personally important to the couple. The following examples may help to give you an idea of the many different ways in which altars can be used.

This lace-covered altar held two small candles representing the two parties entering the marriage, and one large candle that symbolizing the marriage itself. There were also two much smaller candles to signify the family planned for the future. On one side stood a decanter of wine and a single goblet. These were used as part of a blessing during the ceremony. On the other side was a loaf of bread, also a part of the rite. On either end of the altar was a ring and a copy of the personal vow that was made as the ring was given.

This round table was used as a microcosm of the circle, with the four directions and elements within it. Each direction was plotted with a compass, and a different-colored candle was set to mark east, north, west, and south. In the east, the scrolls holding the vows were positioned. The vows, as words, are associated with air, which belongs to the east. In the north, between two rose quartz crystals representing the element of earth, were placed the rings, symbolizing the materializing of the union and the endlessness of the circle. The west held two goblets of wine, used in connection with the element of water to mean compassion and an emotional joining. The south, related to fire, held a vase of red roses that symbolized passion, love, and beauty.

Often the mantle above a fireplace becomes a kind of natural altar. The couple who used this altar were married in their home. They used the altar above the fireplace to honor and interact with their spiritual tradition. None of the religious icons on the altar were actually used during the ceremony, but rather served to lend their energy as sacred objects and to create the feeling tone of a place imbued with spirit. With a brightly burning fire and the wealth of cherished power objects, this was a perfect setting to heighten the feelings of the ceremony.

For an outdoor wedding that took place in a meadow area of a large park, a central altar was constructed that was actively used during the ceremony. All the guests sat surrounding the officiant and the betrothed, who knelt before the the altar. A small fire in a stone pit was the central feature of the altar. Placed around the fire pit were other objects to be used in the ceremony: a box of journal pages, gift-wrapped tokens which the couple exchanged during the ceremony, and rings that were given along with the vows. During the ceremony the couple each took from the box pages on which they had written their fears about marriage and commitment. These fears resulted from previous failed relationships, feelings about the relationships in their families, and knowledge of the difficulties others had experienced. As each fear was read aloud it was given to the fire as a symbol of release.

Multiple Altars

Although not every altar is as useful as the fire altar, each altar can hold a great deal of symbolic significance. While it is not necessary to have an altar at all, and one altar can certainly suffice, there are times or reasons to include more than one.

Mexican *retablos* are folk paintings done on or in metal that are used as center-pieces in personal shrines. This diagram depicts two altars that were made to honor each partner's ancestry as leading to the relationship and family that they were developing. Each member of the couple created an altar using the same basic idea. The central focus was a retablo done in a kind of collage form. Each frame held a family history composed of photographs, photo xeroxes, paintings, writing, and other memorabilia. This was surrounded by flowers, fruits, coins, and other symbols of abundance. In front of each retablo was a small picture frame holding a photograph of the couple taken at their engagement party.

This directional altar was used in an earth-centered ceremony. A circle was laid with bouquets of wild flowers and flower petals. At the periphery of the circle, in each of the four directions was a small altar. A flowing, diaphanous fabric threaded with silver draped every altar. On each table was a lantern with a burning candle, bowls of various types of dried and scented flower petals, burning incense, and special symbols that were personal to the couple. Symbolic items specific to each direction were also laid upon the appropriate altars. These directional altars and the items they held were an integral part of the ceremony.

Group Participation

The altars I have just described were the focal points of a ceremony that also used the symbolism of the circle in a number of ways to actively involve the guests in the ritual. One was with the singing of a chant or round. As you probably know, a round is a short song for more than one voice, in which the second voice starts when the first reaches the second phrase, and so on. The song can be repeated, or "go around," as many times as desired. The round used in this ceremony was a song handed down through women's oral tradition: "Love, love, love, love, / People we are made for love; / Love each other as ourselves, / For we are one."

When the guests have the opportunity to participate in some fashion it seems to make the occasion more meaningful. How you may want your friends and families to participate will be somewhat prescribed by the size of the company. In small weddings it is easy to find a way for everyone to join in. Finding creative ways to use personal or traditional symbols will often provide opportunities for others to participate. You can actually have your friends and family perform the ceremony. Everyone can take a turn talking, reading, or guiding you through parts of the ritual. The officiant will, of course, be present to acknowledge that you are married so that you can have legal recognition of the marriage.

I've performed a number of ceremonies in which the guests participated by offering blessings at some point during the rite. Since a blessing is an offering, connecting the wish with some tangible item is a way to make it more real. You can have guests bring token gifts of a symbolic nature that represent what they wish for you. As they each state their wish and present their gift, you can place it into a special box that can eventually serve as a kind of home altarpiece.

Guests can also offer blessings accompanied by food or wine. In one ceremony each guest made a wish for the couple while pouring some wine from a decanter into a goblet. When all the wishes were made, the bride and groom each took a sip from the cup. In another small wedding this idea was reversed. The couple had been together for quite a while before they finally decided to marry. They felt a great deal of appreciation for all the support their friends and family had shown them over the years. To acknowledge this, they made a blessing over some bread, which they said represented the love and the strength they had received from their real and created families. The bread was *panforte,* a sweet and heavy Italian fruitcake predominantly made with nuts and dried fruits. As a symbol of gratitude and reciprocity, the bread was carried through the room and offered to all present. As another prayer was said, everyone ate their bit of the bread.

Sharing bread or wine or presenting gifts is also a good way to symbolize the separation of parents and children within the ceremony. In the bread sharing ceremony I described in Chapter 3, the parents blessed the bread which they then offered to the couple, symbolically releasing them into a new life together. In a different wedding ceremony, the couple chose to enact the separation from their families of origin by presenting them with special gifts at a particular point in the ritual.

In large weddings, it may seem impossible to have everyone participate, and you may find that it makes more sense just to designate a wedding party. Those selected can be assigned a variety of functions. However, even with a large group there are creative ways to include all the guests, if only for a prayer or meditation. The officiant or some other member of the wedding party can read a prayer or blessing, asking the company to state "Amen" or "And so it is" at the end. Or you can have a special prayer or song printed up. At some point in the ceremony everyone is asked to join in the expression of the piece. The copies can be handed out to the guests before the service, be included in a program, or placed on the seats.

Programs

Speaking of programs, here is another way to add a special touch to your wedding. Essentially a program is a guide to the unfolding of the ceremony. It begins with the basic information that is included in the wedding invitation. This is followed by a kind of schedule that begins with the processional and breaks down the ceremony piece by piece, ending with the recessional. The most creative program I've seen was made to look somewhat like a playbill. It announced the wedding, listed the names of all the participants and the roles they were responsible for, acknowledged those who had provided services, and had other clever distinctions. You might want to use a program if your ceremony is going to be long; include songs, prose, or poetry; require special participation, or have unusual elements you want to explain.

Your programs can be made to match your invitations if you like. Programs can also simply be a printed or handwritten page presented as is or in scroll form.

Marriage Contracts

Another job for the printer or calligrapher is the marriage contract. In the Jewish tradition it was standard to have a contract drawn up that was read at the time of the ceremony.

> In *The Complete Book of Jewish Observance*, Leo Trepp explains that a traditional Ketubah, or marriage contract, delineat[es] the mutual obligations between husband and wife. Among its provisions is the exact amount of money to be paid to the bride in the event of her bridegroom's death or of his divorcing her. Especially among Sephardim (Jews of Spanish-Portuguese origin), the Ketubah was often highly ornamented and decorated with intricate and colorful designs.[4]

A contract can cover any aspect of the relationship. Legal contracts pertain only to money and actual property; if you want a legal contract, you can include a list of your separate and communal properties. But I am more interested in talking about the personal elements of a nonlegal contract. Some couples choose to frame the complete text of the wedding service. Others choose to excerpt the vows from the ceremony and create a special placement for them. Whatever vows you make during the ceremony, you will undoubtedly discover that with time your intentions and your understandings change. Therefore, you may wish to draw up a contract that will call for a periodic reevalutation of your vows. At these times you can devise creative ways to enhance or modify your original promises so they remind you of why you are together, yet allow you both to grow.

Favors

Just as you want to have a living memory of your wedding for yourselves, you may wish also to provide some token for your friends and families that will enable them

to recall the occasion. Favors are often included at traditional ceremor
mal wedding favors may be placed alongside each plate at the dinner. S
may consist of candies specially wrapped or packaged, or matches wit
of the married couple and the date of the wedding printed on the c
couples print their names and the date of the occasion on the top of a little scroll
which may also hold a poem or prayer. A friend showed me a glass dinner bell she
had once received as a favor. It was inscribed with the couple's names and the date,
and had a lace ribbon tied around the bell's handle.

It is not necessary to have a sit-down dinner or a large budget to be able to give
tokens. Some of the nicest remembrances are made by hand. An artist friend made
pins as favors for all the guests at her fortieth birthday. She cut a shape from corru-
gated cardboard, which she painted differently on each side. The front had a special
inscription and some beadwork, while the back had a small brass safety pin attached
to it. Everyone wore their pins during the evening and many saved them afterwards.
This imaginative idea could easily be adapted for a wedding. Or you could use a
photograph taken of the two of you before the wedding to make a favor. One
option might be to insert the photos into hand-cut and painted heart-shaped
frames. You might want to paint your names and the date of your wedding on each
frame. Photographs can also be reproduced as round, button-like pins, which can
later be worn or hung on a bulletin board. Photo finishing shops frequently offer a
number of other creative photo keepsakes. Incorporating photographs into the
favors is a nice way of insuring that your gift will really be a remembrance.

CHAPTER SEVEN

SUSTAINING THE COMMITMENT

H AVING COME THIS FAR, I hope you're ready to develop a wedding that will be one of the high points in your lives. Many couples find that their marriage is made in a state of ecstasy. In many ways earthly love can be a close approximation of heaven. When you are part of a ceremony that is born of love, that symbolizes union and never having to be alone, along with the knowing that you are truly lovable and acceptable, you are filled with an incredible sense of security. What's more, you are likely to have the feeling that the experience is there to stay. I've always said that performing weddings is my favorite job. The abundance of love that flows from the couple and is evoked from the guests washes over me, nourishing and healing me as if it were my own. And in truth, it is. Love is something that belongs to each of us; and weddings are times when we have greater access to this wonder.

Once the wedding ceremony has passed, the euphoria is likely to linger, and then subside. The challenges of daily living can transform the state of love into many more practical expressions. The crucible of reality can turn rapture into constancy. This is the incorporation stage of the wedding ritual, when the true melding that creates the unity of a strong relationship must develop.

Even though this book is touted as a guidebook, there is really no step-by-step guide to having a happy and successful marriage. However, having trained as a marriage and family counselor, and having worked in a therapeutic setting with a good number of couples and families, I do have a few secrets I can share with you. Many of these will be of a practical nature. But before we build resources, let's start with what you already have.

Romance

Chances are, even if you have been together for a number of years before you decide to marry, your wedding will bring renewed feelings of romance to your relationship. If you wed after a short to moderate courtship, you are likely still to be in the honeymoon phase of your relationship. These feelings can be more than just happy memories. There's is a wonderful technique I discovered in a book that I'd like to share with you.

> Every night as you hold each other before sleep, think of what your part-ner has said or done to show you in the course of the day that he or she loves you. It's a simple thing to do.
>
> 'I felt loved by you today. You put a flower in my appointment book, and every time I opened the book, I saw it and felt wonderful.'
>
> 'I felt loved by you today. I know how busy you are, but you called me just to see how I was getting along.'
>
> …In the poem of the marriage bed, very amazing changes begin to occur. You begin to look for ways in which your partner is saying 'I love you' nonverbally. You begin to look for ways to show your love for your partner. Your feelings of being loved grow and grow. Your desire to love in return grows and grows.'

If you can find ways to keep your love alive and vital, it can provide a strong ground that can help you weather differences.

Communication Skills

In some states irreconcilable differences are the only necessary grounds for divorce. I think irreconcilable differences is a concept we should explore. Now differences between *any* two people are a given. I have two younger sisters. There are seven years between Bonnie and me, and six more years between Lori and me. Although we all grew up in the same family, we are very different women. Perhaps this is due to birth order, perhaps it is because we are each a product of the different decades in which we were born. Perhaps we are different because of the ways our parents changed over the years. The source of our differences is unimportant. What does matter is how we've learned to deal with these differences successfully. A primary skill to aid any two people is good communication.

People communicate on several levels simultaneously. Words are enhanced or contradicted by tone of voice, facial expression, body language, and gesture. Even when these elements are all congruent, there is still room for error, as people often have different interpretations of what things mean. Let me give you some examples. When someone asks "Where were you?" with a relaxed posture and a curious expression and tone of voice, the question seems innocent and interested. On the other hand, if someone asks the same question with folded arms, a tapping foot, a clenched jaw, and a tight voice, we infer that the questioner is angry because the questionee has been somehow unavailable.

Then there are differences in understanding. When one person says, "The car needs to be washed," he or she might mean only to observe that the car has gotten rather dirty. Another person, using exactly the same words, may be saying, "You should wash the car now." Words themselves are often unclear. As symbols, words can have many, often contradictory meanings. What does "okay" mean? If you feel okay, does that mean good, no complaints, tolerable, or what?

Effective communication means understanding what you are feeling, and knowing exactly what you want your partner to understand from your message. For example, you might say, "I'm really angry (or depressed, or confused) and I need some time alone before I can talk about this." or, "I need to talk with you, but I want to know if this is a good time for you to be really open and listen to me?" As a receiver, you need to know how to ask for clarification of messages that are confusing or contradictory, and to ask in a noncritical fashion. It is perfectly okay to say, "I'm not sure I understand what you want from me," or "When you say (or do) _____, I feel like _____. Was that your intention?" Getting your needs met in a mutually acceptable way can be simple (if there is no underlying issue at hand). The book *Marital Therapy* recommends beginning requests with phrases like "'I would appreciate it if you would...' or 'I would like you to...' or simply 'Would you please....' The second clause of the request must be stated in specific and neutral language so that the listener knows exactly what is being asked of him/her."[2]

Many communication problems come from the different ways people have of defining things. Just as some people prefer classical music while others like blues, and some people know they are finished with their meal because they feel full while others are done when the plate is empty, we all have our own ways of being in the world. Many of these are defined during childhood. Our feelings and behaviors may be so ingrained that we do not even recognize them. But if you were raised in a family where anger was not directly expressed and your mate comes from a group of people who got things off their chests whenever and however they pleased, you two may have some balancing to do. Your conscious and unconscious beliefs will come into play in the dance of relationship.

Roles and Rules

Once two people join in a relationship they become part of a dynamic system. A system is like a whole other entity. It has a life of its own. The system, call it family system, will be created and sustained by each individual's role and rules. You may notice that over time certain patterns develop between you. Some may be overt and agreeable to both of you. Perhaps one of you is skilled with figures and takes the responsibility for the budget, the bills, and balancing the checkbook. You become the family bookkeeper. Your partner may at first be relieved to be free from that job. After a while, you begin to make rules about spending so the budget can be kept. You are just doing a job both of you at first felt good about. Suddenly your partner begins to feel that you are deciding how he or she is to spend money. If you have become an authority figure as well as the bookkeeper, resentment may be directed towards you. If you enjoy making rules and exerting power with respect to finances, you may forsake flexibility. Suddenly there is a covert pattern in your relationship, one that expresses power struggles. Open communication would be necessary here to prevent a destructive trend from taking hold.

Certain rules, roles, and patterns of behavior may be completely welcomed by both of you. Staying in bed Sunday mornings with breakfast and the paper or visiting relatives one afternoon each month is the kind of ritual many people enjoy. But think back a moment to the chapter where I talked about the origin of the various customs that compose traditional weddings. Many things become patterns that have a strong hold even after the original meaning has been lost. Ideas and actions that may be exciting and rewarding at one time in your life can become restrictive and harmful later. Nothing need be continued just for its own sake.

I know one couple who has developed a successful plan to keep their marriage in tune. They get together for one hour every three weeks to touch bases. During this time they discuss any past, present, or future issues they have been carrying. As artists, they use a technique based on drawing and interpreting symbols to help them. For conflicts between them, they each go within and get in touch with what they are feeling. Both then draw a representation of their feelings on a pad of paper. They each, in turn, discuss their own drawing. They then comment on the other's drawing.

The next stage involves focusing on the approaching three weeks. Each partner goes inside and thinks about what is coming up in the next three weeks. They both draw symbol pictures for each week. Again, they each discuss their pictures and their feelings with the other. In the final stage, they review the three weeks that have passed, and compare what they drew and the interpretations of their drawings with what actually occurred. This keeps them involved in each other's lives in an objective fashion.

It does help to have something or someone outside that has some objectivity to help with perspective. This could also be a therapist, or a religious or spiritual adviser. It is not necessary to have a problem to use these forms of assistance. Remember the old adage, "An ounce of prevention is worth a pound of cure." You can, of course, manage this on your own in many instances. One good exercise to help with this is called "Entering another's world." In this exercise you sit in a comfortable chair, close your eyes, and take a few moments to relax and bring your focus inward. Then you imagine that you are becoming your spouse. Suppose that when you wake up the next day, you have been magically transformed into your partner. Visualize that you go through the day, your partner's day, as him or her. Get in touch with what it's like to have another way of being and feeling. This exercise is very good at fostering understanding and tolerance. It builds bridges.

Rapport

Another way to look at this is as a way of building rapport. When two people are in harmony or agreement, they are in rapport. Chances are that you have a lot in common and that is why you chose to marry each other. But take a few minutes to check out these questions. In your family of origin, you were taught many things either with words or actions. What did you learn about what it means to be a man or a woman in the world? How was each of these things expressed or dealt with in your family: anger? love? grief? fear? discipline? What were you taught about your own religious group, racial/ethnic group, socioeconomic group; about other religious, racial/ethnic, and socioeconomic groups; about education, sexuality, work, the importance of the family? These learnings will be a large part of who you are and how you deal with life and with relationship.

Once you have an understanding of where you are coming from, you have more options about where you are going. When you find that someone you really love has different ideas or behaviors than you do, you each have an opportunity to evaluate what is going on. You can each move toward another way of thinking. You can find common ground. As you explore and review your beliefs, you can also keep your goals for your relationship fresh.

In generations past the success of a marriage was determined by its longevity. But managing to stay together for fifty years is not necessarily an indication that a couple has achieved satisfaction. A strong marriage is a growing force that is composed of many things. There must be friendship, respect, affection, nourishment, trust, forgiveness, dependability, compromise, tolerance, and love. As these things develop and deepen between you, the substance of your relationship produces increasing fulfillment. You may have all the components for a rewarding marriage or you may still be building your cache. Start by identifying and enhancing the behaviors that you find give strength to the relationship. Let the commitment between you form the container that can hold whatever else may come.

Intimacy

In the previous chapter I talked about the symbolism of the circle. In many traditions the circle is used to create a container for a rite. It is used to hold the experience that will take place with safety and protection. Once you have committed to each other, your marriage becomes a kind of container. Because you have vowed to remain together and work through whatever may arise, you have a permission with each other. This works as a safeguard, allowing you to drop your defenses and be more vulnerable. This intimacy you develop can help you understand yourself and your partner more fully.

Francis Dreher and others at the Institute for Educational Therapy in Berkeley, California, have compiled some useful suggestions for achieving intimacy. The teaching text used at the Institute explains that in order to have an intimate relationship you must:

> have enough self-worth to know that you deserve closeness, care, and attention. This means you don't have to play games to get attention. You can ask directly for what you need. It also means you can appreciate each other, can laugh together, can trust each other, share feelings with each other, and share a spiritual connection. People who are intimate can spend time with each other, take turns being the 'leader' in the relationship, and have a relationship full of energy. The following are ways to develop intimacy.

Share Feelings
Take time each day to talk to each other about feelings.
Learn to identify nuances in feelings.
Take the risk of being vulnerable.

Arguments
Talk about what is bothering you (trusting the other to listen).
Stick with an issue until it's resolved and then, let it go.

Get to the feelings behind the issues.
Fight constructively and fairly.
Let go of 'having to be right.'

Promote Closeness
Enjoy nonsexual touch.
Decide what is 'private business' for each of you, and as a couple.
Choose special times to be together.
Have fun together.

Develop Self Worth
Make a realistic assessment of yourself.
Decide on new behaviors and feelings you might want.
Learn to change old programming and behaviors.
Make sure your values and behaviors match.[3]

As months and years pass, both of you will grow in a number of ways. I remember when I was a child in second grade. The school bus picked me up every morning and dropped me off every afternoon. The bus route wound around the different blocks in several directions before finally dropping us at the front door of the school. Once inside the school, a three-story building that covered, at most, half a city block, second graders went directly to their first floor rooms. It was quite a passage to be promoted to the next grade on another floor and wing of the building. One summer I decided to show a visiting cousin my school. This seemed such a formidable journey that we took our compasses and packed a knapsack with vittles to sustain us during the long trip.

Eventually I left that school and even that part of the city. One day, as a young adult visiting my parents, I was sent to fetch my youngest sister who had come down with a fever at school—the same school I had gone to. I drove the mile from my parents' house to the school in less than ten minutes. I walked through the double doors into a hallway lined by tiny lockers. For a moment I was somewhat bewildered. Then I realized what had happened. I'd grown up.

It's interesting to think back on your childhood or adolescence and see how you've grown and how you've stayed the same. All the events of your life are opportunities. Your growth and development come from how you are able to negotiate each trial. Marriage is a supreme test, which means it is also an outstanding opportunity. Whenever the conditions or environment around you changes you are compelled to find ways to continue your growth. Think of yourself as being like a plant. Once a friend who had a luxurious coleus plant gave me a cutting to take home. I kept the piece in water until it rooted. Then I transferred it to some potting soil in a small container and placed it on the windowsill in my office. After awhile, I noticed the plant was becoming spindly. I tried moving it to another location. There it began to lean into the light and eventually it filled out. So, if you are born a coleus you will remain a coleus throughout your life. But the quality of your life can change depending on where and how you live, and your relationship with your environment. You always have choices. There is not necessarily a right choice or a wrong choice for any given situation. However, there are consequences. If a choice does not bring the results you had hoped for, you can always make adjustments.

Behavior Modification

Earlier I mentioned the idea of framing your vows and reviewing them from time to time. The same notion can be applied to the marriage contract, if one was written. Contracts are commonly used in behavior modification, which is a form of therapy based on the work of B. F. Skinner. This approach provides techniques to "modify behaviors" by applying principles of learning. You can learn to change behaviors that are under voluntary control. The best way to do this is with reinforcement. Positive reinforcement rewards a behavior with something pleasurable. For example, one partner might decide to step up a fitness program and go for a run each morning. He or she gets up early, feeds the dog, and the two go out for thirty minutes. The other partner, pleased to have a whining dog out of the house, decides to fix breakfast as an expression of appreciation. Behavior can also be changed by negative reinforcement, when a behavior is altered to end an unpleasant experience. For example, a partner who is chronically late, and comes home to a frustrated mate and an argument, may decide to call home whenever he or she will be over fifteen minutes past schedule. This change in behavior effectively puts a stop to the arguments which had taken the place of a greeting.

Behavior modification can be effectively used in written negotiations. A written contract can help each of you clarify your needs and expectations. Even when you don't have any particular problems, this can be a good way to negotiate busy schedules. For example, one partner writes: I agree to spend one evening finishing the project in the basement. The other partner writes: "I agree to devote Saturday mornings to us." Both sign the agreements. Each should make it as easy as possible for the other to fulfill his or her promise, and specifically acknowledge the other for doing so. If a promise does not get fulfilled, both need to discuss what the obstacles were during the next meeting. Promises should be designed so that they can easily be kept.

Over the years many promises will be made. Some will be broken, many will be kept. If you have marriage meetings every so often, you may want to keep a journal in which you record the details of your process. Looking back over your journal may be a valuable practice. It can also be a source for material you may want to use one day in another ceremony. In the next chapter, we will look at reaffirming your vows.

CHAPTER EIGHT

THE CYCLES OF LOVE: ANNIVERSARIES AND REAFFIRMING VOWS

"EVERYONE DREAMS all the time. There are daydreams, night dreams, dreams of the future...."[1] As a society we are future-oriented. We like to think about what if and what could be.

Perhaps you can remember back to the first time you ever fell in love. I mean way back, to when falling in love meant having a crush on a teacher, or neighbor, or movie star. Chances are you spent a good deal of time in reverie, musing about how your life would magically transform once you were united with this wonderful person. If you are one of the imaginative people who created and maybe even lived in those fantasies, it's likely you've had hopes and dreams about married life, too. Whether you are now planning your first marriage or the last of a series, whether you've been together for a lifetime or just months, you probably have some dreams about how your lives together will unfold. We can plan the future, but we can't predict it. Life always has a way of foisting unexpected changes on us. As the saying goes, the only constant is change.

In the exceptional book, *The Circle of Life*, the circle of the title refers to a developmental or evolutionary wheel. This wheel is divided into four quadrants.

The cusp that represents birth begins the quadrant of childhood. Ninety degrees from birth is the cusp of initiation, from which adolescence develops. Marriage opens the quadrant of adulthood. And death begins the process of remembrance.[2] Within these universal transitional periods we undergo numerous passages. There are births, birthdays, graduations, weddings, anniversaries, promotions, moves, illnesses, deaths, and others. Some are personal, some cultural, and some global. We celebrate or support most of these passages with some sort of ritual.

People in general are oriented toward habit and ritual. We like to ritualize behaviors. It makes us feel good and gives us a sense of continuity and tradition. In your years together you will undoubtedly go through many passages and create many traditions. You may also find that as you grow you relinquish certain traditions that become outmoded. The ways in which you develop as individuals will influence the definition of your marriage. The changes you can go through can be the source for new rituals that will add depth to the bond between you. Over the years, you may wish to create ceremonies to express gratitude for the life you've built together. Or you may want to reaffirm your vows every so often, to make sure your understanding of your commitment reflects your current needs and feelings.

Anniversaries

You can create ceremonies on the anniversaries of your wedding, or at any time you choose. Yearly anniversaries are markers. Tradition has it that certain gifts are associated with the numbers of years of marriage that have passed. The first anniversary is to be commemorated with paper, the second with cotton, and so on. These long-held but vague associations are not likely to bring any great meaning to your relationship. However, if you would like to use them as a starting point, you can adapt them so that they become personally meaningful to you. First let's look at the list:

YEAR	GIFT	YEAR	GIFT
1	paper	15	crystal
2	cotton	20	china
3	leather	25	silver
4	books	30	pearl
5	wood	35	coral
6	candy	40	ruby
7	wool, copper	45	sapphire
8	bronze	50	gold
9	pottery	55	emerald
10	tin, aluminum	60	diamond

On the first anniversary of your wedding, you may wish to use paper symbolically to write a poem or a special verse about what the marriage has meant to you that year. Or perhaps you would like to give your mate a photograph that has special meaning for the two of you. For the second anniversary you could have something made of cotton, like matching bathrobes, embroidered with your names and even the date. Or you could get plain tee shirts and use fabric paint to make a special design. For the third anniversary a leather photo album of meaningful pictures from the past years highlighted with hand-written captions can be a distinctive gift. The books recommended for the fourth-year commemoration might be "how to" guides that teach you something you've been meaning to learn together.

No matter which year you are celebrating, the gift can show more than a remembrance of the day. When you thoughtfully find a way to personalize the gift, even the smallest momento can become a cherished object. It is particularly fitting to find a way to make the gift and the anniversary celebration itself speak to what the relationship means to you.

I know one couple whose unique approach to their wedding became the basis for a yearly tradition. Just before their wedding, they took a two-week vacation in a secluded spot, where they explored what kinds of issues might come up between them and developed their vows. Then, at each anniversary, they returned to the spot to spend quiet time alone together. They used the haven to celebrate, rest, be playful, and evaluate their relationship.

Another couple who had a small wedding with about twenty guests decided to make their fifth anniversary into a kind of reunion. They sent out invitations reminiscent of those used for their wedding. At the party, the videotape of the original ceremony was shown, and everyone shared their recollections of the event. An anniversary cake was adorned with the decorations saved from the wedding cake. Highlighting the event was the recommitment ceremony the couple performed. The whole ritual was again recorded by a videographer, with promises for another party five years hence.

A Michigan couple had a plan to build their dream house. In the first year they worked out the design for the home. Over the years, as they saved for this special home, they commemorated each anniversary by giving each other a unique piece of furniture or other item that would eventually join them there. They literally built a future together.

Of course, for many couples, the future means building a family. There are numerous ways to include children, or planned children, in an anniversary celebration. Family is important in many ways. I found that when I became an adult I was interested in the story of my family. I could spend hours with my parents looking at old pictures and hearing stories about the past. Children love stories. A favorite story for many children is how they came about. This could go something like, "We were all looking forward to your arrival. You were supposed to come at the beginning of August, but you fooled us and came two weeks early...." Another story your children can enjoy is how the two of you fell in love and got married. If the "marriage story" is told at every anniversary, eventually the children will be able to join in the telling. In later years, they will be able to pass this gift to their own children.

There are many rituals that can symbolize the growing relationship between the two of you, and at the same time include others. The one-pot meal is a way to acknowledge nurturing. For the first anniversary you start with either an empty pot or a soup base. Each of you brings an ingredient which represents something you've received from the marriage that year. To start you could use something like miso for fullness and green onions for zest. The second year, each partner adds two ingredients, the third year three, and so on. Eventually this could be a hearty stew or casserole. Of course the dish would be a primary component of the anniversary dinner.

Marriage has a social as well as a personal meaning. Some couples choose to acknowledge this in some fashion in their wedding ceremony. The officiant might say, for example, "Even as your love for each other empowers you individually through your relationship, the power of your relationship should serve as a source of common energy. The strength and esteem nourished in your marriage can be turned outward to the world, beginning a cycle of reciprocity. This is one of the gifts of love—that it increases as it is used." Couples who acknowledge and support these sentiments can use them as a basis for acts that will honor the anniversaries of their years together. Known in some traditions as a "giveaway," a charitable act or gift can be the focus of an anniversary ritual in which you give some of the love the two of you share to the community or the world. You can plant a tree together, perform some community service, or make a donation in your names or in the name of love.

Love was there when you married, and in one form or another you can find it on anniversaries. Sometimes small reminders help. Couples save a piece of the wedding cake in the freezer for the first anniversary. Some couples have preserved flowers from the ceremony by drying or pressing them. Other mementos, like the signatures and best wishes from your guest register, cards that accompanied gifts, or photographs of the ceremony, can all be used as parts of anniversary rituals. The ceremony itself, or the vows made within it, can also provide material for a meaningful anniversary.

Reaffirming Vows

There are many meaningful ways in which vows can be used. You may choose to reaffirm your vows from time to time. Your vows may have taken one of a number of forms. On the one hand, you may have simply responded to the officiant's questions. The officiant may simply have asked, "Do you take _____ to be your husband (wife)?" Whereupon you replied, "I do." Or maybe the officiant asked something broad and encompassing, such as, "_____, do you love _____?" and after your response queried, "Will you care for and support _____ as his wife (her husband)?" On the other hand, you may have written many-faceted vows together, and each of you took a turn stating them or agreeing to them. Or you may have each had different and personal vows that you either read or stated extemporaneously. If your vows were one of the first two types, you will need to approach a recommitment somewhat differently than if they took one of the latter two forms. In either case, a recommitment calls for a reevaluation.

I recently spoke with a woman with an upcoming anniversary. Several years ago she married a man who was a number of years younger, in what is sometimes referred to as "a marriage of necessity." With the third anniversary approaching, this couple has found that although they truly care for each other, they are not well suited. For now they are choosing to remain together so their child can enjoy an intact family. Parenthood and time have taught them a number of skills that allow them to have a satisfactory relationship.

In talking with this woman it seemed an anniversary celebration would not really be appropriate, but a recommitment ceremony just might be. I proposed that each partner spend some time making lists. One list would include all the things they each liked about the other. Another page would enumerate all the strengths and resources they had as a family. The third would concentrate on issues or obstacles.

When the lists were completed they got together to discuss and combine them. Both felt it would be beneficial to include the feelings they originally had for each other, the reasons they fell in love. They decided to begin the ceremony by relating the story of their meeting and the feelings they shared back then. This led to exchanging appreciation for each other and for the family they had created. Next came compromises both were willing to make to nurture and improve the relationship. As a symbolic gesture they exchanged coupon books they had made. Coupons could be redeemed for things like help with the laundry, an hour of peace, an afternoon of babysitting, and so on. The finale was a special dinner.

One woman told me she had remarried a man she had divorced some years earlier. In their second marriage they wanted to try a different approach. After the ceremony they adjourned to a private room along with the officiant. There the three of them worked out a contract. The couple decided they would reevaluate the relationship and update the contract on a yearly basis. They felt this was a realistic way of insuring a long and successful marriage. To further inspire them, they used a quote from T. S. Eliot on the front page of the contract.

With the drawing of this Love and the voice of this calling

> We shall not cease from exploration
> And the end of all our exploring
> Will be to arrive where we started
> And to know the place for the first time....
> And all shall be well and
> All manner of thing shall be well
> When the tongues of flame are in-folded
> Into the crowned knot of fire
> And the fire and the rose are one.[3]

Why would *you* want to reaffirm your vows? Let's say you had written elaborate vows for your wedding. As the years pass you might want to see if you've been able to fulfill the pledge you made. If so, you might consider a ceremony to acknowledge the ease and harmony of your relationship. In the ceremony you can reaffirm the same vows you originally made. One example of this type of ritual contained elements from Native American tradition. The wedding included drumming, sacred songs, and storytelling. Offerings were made to the ancestors whose blessings were requested. The couple had written their vows together in the form of a chant. "You are my beloved, I will always cherish you. You are my beloved, I see your great beauty. You are my beloved, I feel your great power. You are my beloved, I respect your great wisdom. You are my beloved, my home is with you. You are my beloved, I value your independence. You are my beloved, I am radiant in your love. I will always love you. I will always love you. I will always love you." The vows were spoken and echoed line by line.

After several years of marriage this couple made a move to another state. They felt they were starting over and decided it was a good time to bring a sense of stability to their lives. The ceremony was one of the first things they did in their new home. In it, they transplanted a small tree they had taken from the yard of their previous dwelling. Both said a prayer for the tree, and to Spirit. They repeated the vows they had made to each other years earlier, and ended the ceremony with a song from the Keres Indians:

I add my breath to your breath

That our days may be long on the Earth

That the days of our people may be long

That we may be one person

That we may finish our roads together

May our mother bless you with Life

May our Life Paths be fulfilled.

There are a number of reasons you might want to reaffirm your vows. Rituals tend to direct energy toward a larger goal. They bring a balance of material and spiritual energies. Personalized ceremonies also create a sense of continuity and tradition. Couples whose marriages flourish over the years will probably have consciously or unconsciously created special rituals that they regularly carry out. Love can age and grow richer and more mellow, just like a fine wine. Even with long-time friends, the love softens with comfort and deepens with tenderness. Acknowledging and honoring these feelings can enhance the relationship.

Weddings are times of joy and sentiment. Reviewing photographs or film of the day is likely to rekindle many of the feelings of that time. A recommitment ceremony can fulfill a similar function. Some couples like to share this gift with their children once the children have grown old enough to appreciate the experience. Other couples just want to give this gift to themselves over and over again.

One elderly couple who had been married over twenty years began a tradition almost accidentally. Although they'd had a traditional wedding, after the ceremony they had exchanged some special vows of their own. The wife stitched them into a sampler, and the husband made a wooden frame to hold them. For several years, the vows hung in their bedroom. Then, when they were changing things around one year, the hanging was replaced with something else and it was carefully packed away. One afternoon a few more years down the road, the husband was searching through some old files stored in the basement. In one of the boxes he came across the vows. Rereading them together, both were moved and excited. "Let's have another wedding," he said. "Why not just make up our own?" said she. They agreed. Together they made up a short ceremony in which they reaffirmed their vows to one another. They enjoyed themselves so much that they promised to create a new ceremony every year, yet repeat the same vows.

Now there will be some folks who will find that they were not able to completely fulfill their vows. In assessing the obstacles assigning blame is not of value. However, determining realistic alternatives may be. Either partner, at any time, may find they are not fully equipped to deal with the circumstances of life in the best possible way. Stressors may occur within or outside of the marriage that do not respond to the available resources. Promises that were made with the best intentions may be forgotten or broken. This type of situation indicates that some sort of healing is necessary.

Sometimes couples make it through adverse times and are stronger for the experience. Other times the difficulties can drain everyone to the point where the energy of the marriage itself is weakened. But love itself is a healing force.

One couple found that their relationship had languished when one partner was in a long recovery from a bad accident. A positive intervention was needed. They decided to call the friend who had officiated at their wedding to aid them. This friend helped them with a Navaho healing chant:

> Happily I recover.
> Happily my interior becomes cool.
> Happily I go forth.
> My interior feeling cool, may I walk.
> No longer sore, may I walk.
> As it used to be long ago, may I walk.
> Happily, with abundant dark clouds, may I walk.
> Happily, with abundant showers, may I walk.
> Happily, with abundant plants, may I walk.
> Happily, on a trail of pollen, may I walk.
> Happily, may I walk.

Finally, I'd like to share a special recommitment ceremony with you. This one was done by the same officiant that had performed the wedding. It went like this:

Officiant. We are gathered here today to celebrate with _____ and _____ as they reunite in marriage. This is a beautiful and joyous occasion because it acknowledges their commitment in deep friendship and love. This is not a new union, but one that has been tested, matured, and evolved over time.

With this knowing and understanding of each other, you have decided to reaffirm your commitment to spend your lives together. This partnership has allowed you to grow and become aware of yourselves as unique individuals, united in the oneness of love. And it is here today that we honor this. The beauty of your love is that you can each respect the individuality of the other, allowing the freedom that is necessary if we are truly to be ourselves.

One of the beautiful things about this marriage is that while you unite to become one, you do not thereby become less yourselves but more. For this is a union of true freedom, not possessiveness. You each have valuable qualities which you bring to this marriage, and as you treasure your own uniqueness, and that of your partner, your relationship is elevated to that of a true, spiritual union.

How can you become one without losing your individuality? How can you maintain your individuality without distracting from your unity? The answer is to be found in unconditional love, which you have. In love you surrender yourselves, each giving yourself to the other. But you do not lose yourself in the other; you find yourself. You are one, yet you are distinct. That is the paradox, the mystery of love.

The loving relationship you continue to nurture will flow out of that love. It will be for you both, and for everyone whose lives you touch, a thing of beauty and joy forever. (*Each guest passes a rose to the officiant, who gathers them with a ribbon and hands them to the couple.*)

Aware that there is one presence and power, and that we are each part of that unity, we now join in blessing _____ and _____ in the continuing of their lives together. We recognize that the presence of Spirit within them enables them to fulfill the promise of true partnership in life. We know and affirm that they live in joy and in love.

(*The officiant takes their hands in hers.*) May the blessings of life, the joy of love, the peace of truth, the wisdom and strength of Spirit, be your constant companions . . . now and always.

CHAPTER NINE

SAMPLES

I N THIS CHAPTER I would like to present a number of ideas that you can use for inspiration. You will find segments of ceremonies, and creative ideas. The first sample is a fairly complete and somewhat unusual ceremony.

Soft music is playing in the background. The officiant stands at an altar in the front of the room. Ushers lead the guests into the ritual space and seat them on either side of an aisle. The officiant rings bells, then lights two sticks of incense. These are given to two attendants, who walk from the altar and place the sticks in holders near the entry. They also dim the lights. Another two attendants then enter the room, each carrying a lit candle. They approach the altar and stand at either side. The first two attendants return to the altar, also carrying lit candles. They separate and stand beside the others. There is a pause. The *bride and groom enter together, each carrying a tall white candle which is burning brightly, and begin to walk up the aisle.*

Officiant. 'From every human being there rises a light that reaches straight to heaven. And when two souls that are destined to be together find each other, their streams of light flow together, and a single brighter light goes forth from their united being.'[1]

When the couple reaches the altar, they light a large central candle with their two flames, then both place their individual candles in holders to either side of the marriage candle. Each attendant speaks while placing a candle on a corner of the altar.

First attendant. May the light of love...

Second attendant. And the light of understanding...

Third attendant. And the light of respect...

Fourth attendant. And the light of tolerance...

Attendants in unison. Shine eternally for you both. *The attendants step back as the room lights are raised slightly.*

Officiant. Welcome 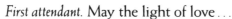 and _____, you have come here today to join your lives in marriage. When we talked, you both said that you felt your coming together and your being together was destined. From the story you shared with me, it seems as if your meeting was indeed a numinous event. Would you now like to relate the tale to the company?

The bride and groom take turns telling the story of their meeting.

Officiant. A striking feature of your relationship is that love was not mentioned in the usual way. You said you felt a recognition and a familiarity with each other. In only a short time the compatibility between you was so deep and so natural you felt as if you had always known each other. This type of knowing and being known is something that generally comes with years of intimacy. Yet the two of you had a natural intimacy that seems to have preceded and perhaps formed the profound love you now share. It is rare to find such abundance. It is rare to have more than enough of something as precious as love.

But even as the measure of love between you is great, the love that surrounds you is greater. At this time the members of your families would like to offer you their blessings. *The parents and siblings from both families come forward one at a time. Each relative joins hands with the bride and groom as they offer a blessing for the marriage. When this has been completed the bride and groom speak some extemporaneous words on the value of family.*

Officiant. Your words have made the value of family quite evident. And I know you are looking forward to beginning your own family in the next few years. This bowl of earth represents the container of your marriage, filled with the richness of creation and nurturing. Would you now like to plant these bulbs which symbolize the new life you wish to bring forth? *Together they plant two bulbs. The officiant places her hands over their hands as they hold the bowl and makes a blessing.* May the spirit of life bless these bulbs and help them grow in strength and beauty.

Officiant. At this time would you express your vows to each other?

Each partner has written a personal sentiment. After the readings, rings are exchanged as each speaks in turn. Accept this ring as a symbol of my everlasting love for you.

Officiant. With the exchange of vows and rings, and the witnessing of this company, you have performed the ceremony that has made you husband and wife. May your lives together be good, and always inspired with the love of this day.

The bride and groom take turns reciting "Love's Philosophy," by Percy Bysshe Shelley.

The fountains mingle with the river,
   And the rivers with the Ocean;
The winds of Heaven mix forever
   With a sweet emotion;
Nothing in the world is single;
   All things by a law divine
In one spirit meet and mingle.
   Why not I with thine?—

See the mountains kiss high Heaven,
   And the waves clasp one another;
No sister-flower would be forgiven
   If it disdained its brother;
And the sunlight clasps the earth,
   And the moonbeams kiss the sea:
What is all this sweet work worth
   If thou kiss not me?[2]

They kiss.

Officiant. To make good use of the love that has been evoked here today, I ask that you all "pass the peace." *Everyone turns to those around them and exchanges a hug or a handshake.*

The music starts up and the now-married couple retreats to the anteroom.

One couple chose two pair of friends who had marriages that they felt were exemplary. These friends were asked to perform the ceremony. The legal aspect of the wedding took place at city hall first thing in the morning. The couple then returned to their home and put the finishing touches on the decorations for the ritual. Friends and families arrived bearing both gifts and food for a potluck celebration. The designated couples and the newlyweds stood before the group. Both of the long-married twosomes talked about what they felt marriage meant and how they had made their marriages successful. These four took turns asking the "will you's" and "do you's." After the vows and ring exchange the couple turned to the group of friends and family and asked, "Will you all promise to be there for us and support us in times of sorrow as well as in times of joy?" The congregation responded in the affirmative. "Then as our first act as a married couple, we invite you to share a glass of wine and a blessing with us." This led to general partying and merriment.

Another couple met when the man, seeking instruction in German, responded to an ad the woman had placed offering tutoring. The differences in their cultures, and the fact that German had brought them together, influenced their decision to have the ceremony conducted in both languages. The officiant read a paragraph or two in English, and an interpreter repeated the words in German. The couple recited their vows in both languages. For the closure, the officiant was given a phonetic translation of the text and was able to say the words in German as well as in English. Here's how it went:

As _____ and _____ have made their vows to each other, formalizing in our presence the existence of the bond between them, we bear witness to the ceremony they have performed that has made them husband and wife. Go out and live and love together.	Da _____ und _____ sich ihr Versprechen gegeben und so in unserer Gegenwart die Existenz des Bandes zwischen ihnen bekundet haben, sind wir Zeugen der Zeremonie, die sie zu Mann und Frau macht. Nun geht und lebt und liebt gemeinsam.

The couple had written their vows in a journal in both languages, and read from the pages during the ceremony. At the end of the ceremony they invited the guests to take a moment at some time during the reception to sign the book and write in any blessing they might have for the couple.

You may recognize this couple from the previous chapter. They spent the two weeks just before their wedding in a secluded spot on a kind of vision quest. Historically and cross-culturally, passages have been supported with transformation rituals. An initiation requires a period of seclusion during which instruction is received. Afterwards a ceremony reunites initiates with the old life in a new way. A marriage can be interpreted as an initiation as it is an entry into a new life with new identities. This couple used their retreat to explore their relationship and discover what issues might come up in their marriage, developing vows that would acknowledge the strengths of the relationship and encourage creative ways of dealing with difficulties. During the two weeks they attempted to live their vows. When they returned they were essentially married. The ceremony was more or less a celebration of their new status.

Another couple was getting married for the second time. Both had children from the earlier marriages. All the children were invited to come up to the altar and share their feelings about the wedding that was occurring and the new family that was forming.

In this ceremony, the guests were given copies of songs and chants as they entered the ritual space. The officiant began the ceremony by asking the company all to sing a simple but touching love song the couple had chosen. At the first chorus, the processional began. Everything was timed so the wedding party would all be standing at the altar by the time the song was completed. At various points in the ceremony, the guests were again asked to join in with singing or chanting.

In a nature-centered wedding a solo flautist led the guests down a path to a meadow where the ceremony was to take place. Everyone formed a circle around an altar which held smoking sage and cedar. The couple entered the circle and walked around it greeting everyone as they passed. Coming to the center of the circle, they used the herbs for a ritual cleansing. One by one the guests stepped into the circle and walked up to the altar. Each guest had brought a token gift, something he or she had made or purchased, that symbolized a wish for the couple. One person offered a miniature papier-mâché basket of fruit to represent abundance.

Another brought a small rose-quartz heart to symbolize love. A family member contributed a link necklace to symbolize the interconnection of family. A box of crayons represented a wish for creative expression. Security was symbolized by a child's bank, wisdom and knowledge with a key and a book, and long-lasting happiness with a bundle of dried flowers. All the gifts were put into a cut-glass box that would allow them to be viewed, and the guests asked to later write a brief summary of their wishes on small cards. The cards would be strung through a ribbon tied around the box, which would have a place of honor in the home of the newlyweds.

After a common prayer, vows were made and rings were exchanged. The ceremony ended with everyone joining in on a song led by the officiant.

Young people in the sixties had what could be called a more idealistic view of the world. We strove to break away from the consensual interpretation of reality. Those known as "flower children" were free-spirited and loving folk who really hoped to change the world and make it a better place. Partly this was attempted with a more childlike recognition and enjoyment of beauty. People who recall weddings from that time get a dreamy look on their faces. In remembered ceremonies friends participated by playing flutes, guitars, and percussive instruments. Complete ceremonies were sometimes totally extemporaneous. The couple might have been surrounded by showers of soap bubbles throughout the rite. Vows were often long, self-written, and poetic. Some ceremonies consisted of nothing more than the reading of verse or certain meaningful stories. Balloons with wishes written upon them were released into the sky. (This is no longer recommended, as it poses environmental hazards.) Singing, dancing, and feasting may have been part of the ceremony itself. Children and pets were not only welcome but frequently active participants. Wedding attire often took on the idea of costume. And good times were had by all.

Two lovers, both jewelers, crafted silver lockets to be used for the token exchange, forsaking the tradition of rings. Into each was placed a ringlet of hair, a sigh, and words of love. Secured and placed on silver chains, the filled charms were exchanged to seal the vows. Wine was shared from a silver chalice. This was an evening ceremony, performed in the light of a full moon. The closing statement was excerpted from a poem by Sylvia Plath.

> From this holy day on, all pollen blown
> Shall strew broadcast so rare a seed on wind
> That every breath, thus teeming, set the land
> Sprouting fruit, flowers, children most fair in legion
> To slay spawn of dragon's teeth: speaking this promise,
> Let flesh be knit, and each step hence go famous.[3]

One couple used a variation on the New Orleans ritual of the "king cake" to replace two rituals that take place at the end of many weddings. Generally the bride tosses her bouquet to the single women to predict the next who will marry, and the groom flings the bride's garter to the single men for the same purpose. This couple made two panettone-type cakes into which tokens were baked. Each cake, ring-shaped itself, held a single band of an inexpensive metal, and was decorated in bright colors with gaudy designs. The two cakes were cut so that the number of slices matched the number of single male and female participants. Whoever received the two slices containing the rings would be the next to marry.

At this ceremony the guests were seated in a semicircle. The betrothed stood before the guests and shared the feelings they held for each other. When they finished speaking they invited the guests to recount their stories of meeting the couple, along with any feelings they had for or about them and the marriage. There was a pause between each speaker to give everyone time to reflect upon what had been said and to give the next speaker time to collect his or her thoughts. After almost an hour of stories, the guests were invited to inscribe their names on a witness scroll. Children and adults alike proudly entered their names.

If you have some practice that is particularly meaningful in your life, you may want to incorporate something from it into your ceremony. You may even want to base your ceremony on the symbols and values associated with your practice. For example, people who identify themselves as ACA's (Adult Children of Alcoholics) grew up in families where alcoholism was prevalent. Chances are a happy childhood was not easily found in such families, and statistics show that children of alcoholics are likely to develop the same condition. Many people go through twelve-step programs such as Alcoholics Anonymous to free themselves from addictive patterns. This work often becomes so important that it causes major lifestyle shifts.

One man who identifies himself as a recovering alcoholic chose to use elements of this recovery work in his wedding. The Serenity Prayer was included in the ceremony. It goes like this: "God, grant me the serenity to accept the things I cannot change; the courage to change the things I can; and the wisdom to know the difference." Perhaps as a way of honoring the inner child, this couple also selected a passage from the book *The Velveteen Rabbit* to use in their vows:

'What is REAL?' asked the Rabbit one day . . . . 'Does it mean having things that buzz inside you and a stick-out handle?'

'Real isn't how you are made,' said the Skin Horse. 'It's a thing that happens to you. When a child loves you for a long, long time, not just to play with, but REALLY loves you, then you become Real. It doesn't happen all at once. You become. It takes a long time. Generally, by the time you are Real, most of your hair has been loved off, and your eyes drop out and

you get loose in the joints and very shabby. But these things don't mat'
at all, because once you are Real you can't be ugly, except to people w
don't understand.'[4]

This excerpt was followed by the statement, "You are Real to me now, and time can
only help me love you more."

In this ceremony two people were marrying each other for the second time.
The woman, escorted by their two children, entered first. The three waited
together as the man stepped toward them carrying a large bouquet of flowers.
When he reached the altar, he withdrew two flowers from the arrangement and
presented each child with one. He then turned towards the bride and placed the
bouquet in her arms as he kissed her, and said: "If a man could pass through Paradise
in a dream, and have a flower presented to him as a pledge that his soul had really
been there, and if he found that flower in his hand when he awoke... what then?"[5]

Together the bride and groom faced the guests and welcomed them. The welcome and most of the ceremony were done as a family. Even the vows had two
parts. First, promises were made by the couple to each other. Next, the family held
hands and vows were made to the children which promised solidarity with and
commitment to being a family again. The couple exchanged rings and a kiss. Then
both children left the altar, and the husband turned towards his wife and recited
the poem entitled "Reprise" by Ogden Nash.

> Geniuses from countless nations
> Have told their love for generations
> Till their memorable phrases
> Are common as goldenrod or daisies.
> Their girls have glimmered like the moon,
> Or shimmered like the summer noon
> Stood like lily, fled like faun,

Now the sunset, now the dawn,
Here the princess in the tower
There the sweet forbidden flower.
Darling, when I look at you
Every aged phrase is new,
And there are moments when it seems
I've married one of Shakespeare's dreams.[6]

Twenty years ago this couple, along with the sister of the bride, performed their own wedding. It began with statements by the bride and groom; then the sister performed most of the ceremony. Towards the end they introduced a judge, who took care of the legal factor.

Bride. Good afternoon, and welcome to our wedding. Well, we've finally decided to do it. We did have some reservations about getting married in a traditional sort of way. In fact, when _____ and I first discussed our wedding, our plan was *not* to have a state-sanctioned or authorized wedding. We don't believe the State has the authority to define and regulate our relationship to each other. We are coming together on our own authority and because we love each other. And it is this love which demands our full responsibility.

Groom. Just as we do not define our marriage to fit specific legal and social outlines, we also choose to redefine the traditional roles of husband and wife. We respect each other as people, and love each other as _____ and _____. We hope always to remain flexible and conscious in our marriage, acting as is appropriate for our needs for a healthy relationship.

Thank you for being here for this unqualified celebration of our love and respect for each other. And now here's _____ [the sister of the bride].

Sister. Good afternoon. Welcome to _____ and _____'s wedding. My name is _____. We have some special people with us today that I would like to introduce to you. (*She names four family members who each briefly stand.*)

_____ and _____, today you are surrounded by your family and friends. We are here to offer you our love and support at this wonderful time, and share in the happiness of this day. We all hope the love you have for each other will continue to grow and flourish, and that your values and dreams can coincide. Through open communication your individual potentials can evolve. Learn to draw from your marriage strength to join together and trust to stand apart.

She offers a series of blessings, then introduces the judge who will officiate for the exchange of vows. Now we are ready to witness the vows you have chosen to love by. We hope they serve as a foundation for a long and healthy relationship. At this time I'd like to introduce _____ [the judge].

Judge, to each partner. Will you have this man (woman) to be your husband (wife), to share your life with: And do you pledge that you will give your love, respect, and tender care through all the varying experiences of your lives? *Each replies in the affirmative.*

At this point rings are exchanged, acknowledgment of the wedding is made, the bride and groom kiss, and as far as I know, they live happily ever after.

For those of you who are now planning your ceremony, may your wedding be filled with joy. "And may your days together be good, and long upon the earth."

CHAPTER TEN
QUOTATIONS AND SONGS

IN THIS CHAPTER you will find some of my favorite and most frequently used quotes. No permission is required to quote a poem or story or to sing a song in a private ceremony. You may already have certain poems or songs that are special to you. Libraries are a good place to do research. There are some books, like *To Woo and to Wed*, edited by Michael Blumenthal and published by Poseidon Press, which are collections of poetry specifically focusing on love and marriage.

Poetry and Prose

I want to beg you, as much as I can, to be patient toward all that is unsolved in your heart and to try to love the questions themselves like locked rooms and like books that are written in a very foreign tongue. Do not seek the answers, which cannot be given you because you would not be able to live them. And the point is to live everything. Live the questions now. Perhaps you will then gradually, without noticing it, live along some distant day into the answer.

RAINER MARIA RILKE
Rilke on Love and Other Difficulties

117

Where the myth fails, human love begins.

ANAÏS NIN

Now you will feel no rain,

For each of you will be shelter to the other.

Now you will feel no cold,

For each of you will be warmth to the other.

Now there is no loneliness for you,

Now there is no more loneliness,

Now there is no more loneliness.

Now you are two persons

But there is one life before you.

Go now to your dwelling place to enter into the days of your togetherness.

And may your days be good and long upon the earth.

APACHE WEDDING BLESSING

Let me not to the marriage of true minds
Admit impediments; love is not love
Which alters when it alteration finds
Or bends with the remover to remove.
O no, it is an ever-fixed mark
That looks on tempests and is never shaken;
It is the star to every wand'ring bark,
Whose worth's unknown, although his height be taken.
Love's not Time's fool, though rosy lips and cheeks
Within his bending sickle's compass come;
Love alters not with his brief hours and weeks,
But bears it out even to the edge of doom.
   If this be error and upon me proved,
   I never writ, nor no man ever loved.

WILLIAM SHAKESPEARE
Sonnet 116

If I speak with the eloquence of men and angels, but have no love, I become no more than blaring brass or crashing cymbal.

If I have the gift of foretelling the future and hold in my mind all human knowledge and if I also have that absolute faith which can move mountains, but have no love, I amount to nothing....

This love of which I speak is slow to lose patience—it looks for a way of being constructive. It is not possessive: it is neither anxious to impose nor does it cherish inflated ideas of its own importance. It is glad when truth prevails. Love knows no limits to its endurance, no end to its trust, no dashing of its hope; it can outlast anything. It is, in fact the one thing that still stands when all else has fallen.

1 CORINTHIANS 13:1 – 2, 4 – 7

Love has no other desire but to fulfill itself.

But if you love and must needs have desires, let these be your desires:

To melt and be like a running brook that sings its melody to the night.

To know the pain of too much tenderness.

To be wounded by your own understanding of love;

And to bleed willingly and joyfully.

To wake at dawn with a winged heart and give thanks for another day of
loving;

To rest at the noon hour and meditate love's ecstasy;

To return home at eventide with gratitude;

And then to sleep with a prayer for the beloved in your heart and a song
of praise upon your lips.

KAHLIL GIBRAN
The Prophet

You were born together, and together you shall be forevermore.

You shall be together when the white wings of death scatter your days.

Ay, you shall be together even in the silent memory of God.

But let there be spaces in your togetherness,

And let the winds of the heavens dance between you.

KAHLIL GIBRAN
The Prophet

For one human being to love another human being: that is perhaps the most difficult task that has been entrusted to us, the ultimate task, the final test and proof, the work for which all other work is but preparation. . . . [Love] is a high inducement for the individual to ripen...to become world in himself for the sake of another person....human love...consists in this: that two solitudes protect and border and greet each other.

RAINER MARIA RILKE
Letters to a Young Poet

When the satisfaction or the security of another person becomes as significant to one as one's own satisfaction or security, then the state of love exists.

HARRY STACK SULLIVAN
Conceptions of Modern Psychiatry

The minute I heard my first love story I started looking for you, not knowing how blind that was. Lovers don't finally meet somewhere. They're in each other all along.

RUMI
The Ruins of the Heart

Love—Eros—makes his home in men's hearts, but not in every heart, for where there is hardness he departs. His greatest glory is that he cannot do wrong nor allow it; force never comes near him. For all men serve him of their own free will. And he whom Love touches not walks in darkness.

PLATO

A contract of eternal bond of love,
Confirm'd by mutual joinder of your hands,
Attested by the holy close of lips,
Strength'ned by interchangement of your rings
And all the ceremony of this compact
Seal'd in my function, by my testimony. . . .

WILLIAM SHAKESPEARE
Twelfth Night V.i. 156–161

In a time when nothing is more certain than change, the commitment of two people to one another has become difficult and rare. Yet, by its scarcity, the beauty and value of this exchange have only been enhanced.

ROBERT SEXTON
"The Vow"

I want to love you without clutching, appreciate you without judging, join you without invading, invite you without demanding, leave you without guilt, criticize you without blaming, and help you without insulting. If I can have the same from you then we can truly meet and enrich each other.

VIRGINIA SATIR
Making Contact

Do not ask me to abandon or forsake you! for wherever you go I will go, wherever you lodge I will lodge, your people shall be my people, and your God my God.

RUTH 1:16

To him who suffers but not for love, to suffer is suffering and hard to bear. But one who suffers for love suffers not, and his suffering is fruitful in God's sight.

MEISTER ECKHART

The web of marriage is made by propinquity, in the day to day living side by side, looking outward and working outward in the same direction. It is woven in space and in time of the substance of life itself.

ANNE MORROW LINDBERGH
Gift from the Sea

n every human being there rises a light that reaches straight to
en. And when two souls that are destined to be together find each
their streams of light flow together, and a single brighter light goes
forth from their united being.

BAAL SHEM TOV

the quiet thoughts
of two people a long time in love
touch lightly
like birds nesting in each other's warmth
you will know them by their laughter
but to each other
they speak mostly through their solitude
if they find themselves apart
they may dream of sitting undisturbed
in each other's presence
of wrapping themselves warmly
in each other's easy

HUGH PRATHER
Notes on Love and Courage

I love you,

Not only for what you are,

But for what I am

When I am with you,

Not only for what

You have made of yourself,

But for what

You are making of me.

I love you

For the part of me

That you bring out;

I love you

For putting your hand

Into my heaped up heart

And passing over

All the foolish, weak things

That you can't help

Dimly seeing there,

And for drawing out into the light

All the beautiful belongings

That no one else had looked

Quite far enough to find.

I love you because you

Are helping me to make

Of the lumber of my life

Not a tavern

But a temple;

Out of the works

Of my every day

Not a reproach

But a song....

ROY CROFT

Grow old along with me!
The best is yet to be,
The last of life, for which the first was made. . . .

ROBERT BROWNING
"Rabbi Ben Azra"

There is only one happiness in life, to love and be loved.

GEORGE SAND
Letter to Lina Calamatta

Love is a state in which one lives who loves, and whoever loves has given himself away; love then, and not marriage, is belonging. Marriage is the public declaration of a man and a woman that they have formed a secret alliance, with the intention to belong to, and share with each other, a mystical estate. . . .

KATHERINE ANNE PORTER
Collected Essays

Come live with me and be my love,
And we will some new pleasures prove,
Of golden sands and crystal brooks,
With silken lines and silver hooks.

JOHN DONNE
"The Bait"

Love alone is capable of uniting living beings in such a way as to complete and fulfill them, for it alone takes them and joins them by what is deepest in themselves.

PIERRE TEILHARD DE CHARDIN

In love the paradox occurs that two beings become one and yet remain two.

ERICH FROMM

It is the true season
of Love
when we know that
we alone can love,
that no one could ever
have loved before us
and that no one
will ever Love
in the same way
after us.

JOHANN WOLFGANG VON GOETHE

Songs

I'm gonna love you
Like nobody's loved you,
Come rain or come shine.
High as a mountain
And deep as a river,
Come rain or come shine.

I guess when you met me
It was just one of those things,
But don't ever bet me,
'Cause I'm gonna be true if you let me.

You're gonna love me
Like nobody's loved me,
Come rain or come shine.
Happy together,
Unhappy together
And won't it be fine.

Days may be cloudy or sunny,
We're in or we're out of the money,
But I'm with you always,
I'm with you rain or shine!

JOHNNY MERCER AND HAROLD ARLEN
"Come Rain or Come Shine"

"Come Rain or Come Shine," from the musical production *St. Louis Woman,* is sung by Ray Charles on Atlantic Records. Other songs you might like to use are "It Had to be You," by Gus Kahn and Isham Jones, performed by Harry Connick, Jr., on the soundtrack of *When Harry Met Sally* (Columbia Records), and "My Forever Love" written by LeVert and Gordon and performed by Gerald LeVert on *Big Throwdown* (Atlantic Records).

Notes

Introduction

1. Lederer and Jackson, *Mirages of Marriage*, 28–29.
2. Jeláluddin Rumi, quoted in Leonard, *Way to the Wedding*, page facing Part 1.
3. van Gennep, *Rites of Passage*, quoted in van der Hart, *Rituals*, 114.
4. de Rougement, *Love in the Western World*, 286.
5. Beck and Metrick, *Art of Ritual*, 5.

Chapter 1. The Need for a Personalized Wedding

1. *Alternative Service Book*, 124. (The quotation in the final sentence is from *Marriage and the Family in Britain Today—A Survey by the Board of Social Responsibility* [London: CIO Publishing, 1974], 8.)
2. Hutton, comp., *Marriage Manual*, 67.
3. Rich, *Dream of a Common Language*, 67.
4. Matthiessen, "Rites that Bind," *San Francisco Examiner*, 20 October 1991.

Chapter 2. Creating a Ritual

1. Sanford, *Healing and Wholeness*, 60.
2. Lacey, *Wedding*, 18, 42.
3. Gibran, *Prophet*, 11.

Chapter 3. Customs, Then and Now

1. *Herder Symbol Dictionary*, v.
2. Sproul, *Primal Myths*, 1, 5.
3. Walker, *Woman's Encyclopedia*, 586.
4. Matlins, Bonanno, and Crystal, *Rings*, frontispiece.
5. Slater, ed., *Pagan Rituals*, 45.
6. Quoted from Cooper, *Traditional Symbols*, 24.
7. *Brides' Book of Etiquette*, 23.

Chapter 4. Planning Your Ceremony

1. Rilke, *Young Poet*, 68–69, 78.
2. Poor, ed., *You and the Law*, 365.

Chapter 5. Details, Details

1. Arisian, *New Wedding*, 113.
2. Yeats, "The Celtic Element in Literature," *Essays and Introductions*, 174.
3. Butler, ed., *Ceremonies*, 225.

Chapter 6. Special Touches

1. Cooper, *Traditional Symbols*, 11.
2. Ibid., 90.
3. Fuller, "Altars of Our Lives," *San Francisco Examiner*, 28 April 1991.
4. Trepp, *Jewish Observance*, 278.

Chapter 7. Sustaining the Commitment

1. Crowther and Stone, *Intimacy*, 147.
2. Jacobson and Margolin, *Marital Therapy*, 167.
3. Dreher et al., teaching text, Institute for Educational Therapy, n.p.

Chapter 8. Anniversaries and Reaffirming Vows

1. Dreher et al., teaching text.
2. Cohen, ed., *Circle of Life*. My description summarizes a diagram in the table of contents.
3. Eliot, *Four Quartets*, 59.

Chapter 9. Samples

1. Baal Shem Tov, quoted in Butler, ed., *Ceremonies*, 290.
2. Shelley, "Love's Philosophy," *English Romantic Writers*, 1028.
3. Plath, "Wreath for a Bridal," *Collected Poems*, 45.
4. Williams, *Velveteen Rabbit*, 16–17.
5. Samuel Taylor Coleridge, *The Notebooks of Coleridge*, ed. Kathleen Coburn, 1956. Quoted in Borges, "The Flower of Coleridge," *Reader*, 164.
6. Nash, "Reprise," *Versus*, 91.

Chapter 10. Quotations and Songs

Quotations of George Sand, Pierre Teilhard de Chardin, and Erich Fromm are from *Love: Quotations from the Heart;* of Plato, from Hamilton, *Mythology;* of Meister Eckhart, from Campbell, *Myths to Live By;* of Baal Shem Tov, from Butler, *Ceremonies of the Heart;* and of Goethe, from Schutz, *Language of Love*. Sources for other quotations are listed under the author's name in "References and Further Reading."

References and Further Reading

The Alternative Service Book. London: CIO Publishing, 1980.

Arisian, Khoren. *The New Wedding.* New York: Vintage, 1973.

Beck, Renee, and Sydney Barbara Metrick. *The Art of Ritual.* Berkeley, Calif.: Celestial Arts, 1990.

Blumenthal, Michael, ed. *To Woo and to Wed.* New York: Poseidon Press, 1992.

Borges, Jorge Luis. *Borges: A Reader.* Edited by Emir Rodriguez Monegal and Alastair Reid. New York: Dutton, 1981.

Bride's Book of Etiquette. 3d ed. New York: Grosset and Dunlap, 1978.

Broadwell, Lynn. *Here Comes the Guide.* Berkeley, Calif.: Hopskotch Press, 1990.

Browning, Robert. "Rabbi Ben Ezra." *Poems of Robert Browning.* Edited by Donald Smalley. Boston: Houghton Mifflin, 1956.

Butler, Becky, ed. *Ceremonies of the Heart.* Seattle, Wash.: Seal Press, 1990.

Campbell, Joseph. *Myths to Live By.* New York: Bantam Books, 1984.

Cohen, David, ed. *The Circle of Life.* San Francisco: Harper, 1991.

Cooper, J. C. *An Illustrated Encyclopaedia of Traditional Symbols.* London: Thames and Hudson, 1978.

Croft, Roy. "I Love You." *The Language of Love.* Edited by Susan Polis Schutz. Boulder, Colo.: Blue Mountain Arts, 1975.

Crowther, C. Edward, and Gayle Stone. *Intimacy.* Santa Barbara, Calif.: Capra Press, 1986.

de Rougemont, Denis. *Love in the Western World.* New York: Schocken Books, 1983.

Donne, John. "The Bait." *The Norton Anthology of English Literature.* Vol. 1. 3d ed. New York: W. W. Norton, 1974.

Dreher, Francis, et al. Instructional material from the Institute for Educational Therapy. Berkeley, Calif., 1991.

Eliot, T. S. *Four Quartets.* New York: Harcourt, Brace and World, 1943.

Fuller, Carol. "Altars of Our Lives." *This World* supplement, *San Francisco Examiner*, 28 April 1991.

Gibran, Kahlil. *The Prophet.* New York: Alfred A. Knopf, 1923.

Hamilton, Edith. *Mythology.* New York: New American Library, 1942.

Herder Symbol Dictionary. Translated by Boris Matthews. Wilmette, Ill.: Chiron Publications, 1986. Originally published as *Herder Lexikon: Symbole.* Freiburg, Ger.: Herder, 1978.

Hutton, Samuel Ward, comp. *Minister's Marriage Manual*. Grand Rapids, Mich.: Baker Book House, 1968.

Jacobson, Neil S., and Gayla Margolin. *Marital Therapy*. New York: Brunner/Mazel, 1979.

Lacey, Peter. *The Wedding*. New York: Ridge Press, 1969.

Lederer, William J., and Don D. Jackson. *The Mirages of Marriage*. New York: W. W. Norton, 1968.

Leonard, Linda Schierse. *On the Way to the Wedding*. Boston: Shambhala, 1986.

Lindbergh, Anne Morrow. *Gift from the Sea*. New York: Random House, 1978.

Love: Quotations from the Heart. Philadelphia: Running Press, 1990.

Matlins, Antoinette, Antonio C. Bonanno, and Jane Crystal. *Engagement and Wedding Rings*. South Woodstock, Vt.: Gemstone Press, 1990. Distributed by Van Nostrand Reinhold, New York.

Matthiessen, Peter. "The Rites That Bind." *Image* magazine, *San Francisco Examiner*, 20 October 1991.

Nash, Ogden. "Reprise." *Versus*. Boston: Little, Brown and Co., 1949.

Plath, Sylvia. "Wreath for a Bridal." *The Collected Poems of Sylvia Plath*. Edited by Ted Hughes. New York: Harper and Row, 1960.

Poor, Henry V., ed. *You and the Law*. Pleasantville, N.Y.: Reader's Digest Association, 1984.

Porter, Katherine Anne. *The Collected Essays and Occasional Writings of Katherine Anne Porter*. New York: Delacorte, 1970.

Prather, Hugh. *Notes on Love and Courage*. New York: Doubleday, 1977.

Rich, Adrienne. *The Dream of a Common Language*. New York: W. W. Norton, 1978.

Rilke, Rainer Maria. *Letters to a Young Poet*. Translated by Stephen Mitchell. New York: Vintage, 1984.

_____. *Rilke on Love and Other Difficulties*. Translated by Stephen Mitchell. New York: Vintage, 1984.

Rumi, Jeláluddin. *The Ruins of the Heart*. Translated by Edmund Helminski. Vermont: Threshold, 1981.

Sanford, John. *Healing and Wholeness*. New York: Paulist Press, 1977.

Satir, Virginia. *Making Contact*. Berkeley, Calif.: Celestial Arts, 1976.

Schutz, Susan Polis, ed. *The Language of Love*. Boulder, Colo.: Blue Mountain Arts, 1975.

Sexton, Robert. "The Vow." *An American Romantic*. Oakland, Calif.: Merit Publications, 1986.

Shakespeare, William. *The Riverside Shakespeare*. Edited by G. Blakemore Evans. Boston: Houghton Mifflin, 1974.

Shelley, Percy Bysshe. "Love's Philosophy." *English Romantic Writers*. Edited by David Perkins. New York: Harcourt Brace Jovanovich, 1967.

Slater, Herman, ed. *A Book of Pagan Rituals*. York Beach, Maine: Samuel Weiser, 1978.

Sproul, Barbara C. *Primal Myths*. San Francisco: Harper & Row, 1979.

Sullivan, Harry Stack. *Conceptions of Modern Psychiatry*. New York: Norton, 1953.

Trepp, Leo. *The Complete Book of Jewish Observance*. New York: Behrman House/Summit Books, 1980.

van der Hart, Onno. *Rituals in Psychotherapy*. New York: Irvington Publishers, 1983.

van Gennep, Arnold. *The Rites of Passage*. London: Routledge and Kegan Paul, 1960.

Walker, Barbara G. *The Woman's Encyclopedia of Myths and Secrets*. San Francisco: Harper & Row, 1983.

Williams, Margery. *The Velveteen Rabbit*. New York: Doubleday, 1991

Yeats, W. B. "The Celtic Element in Literature." *Essays and Introductions*. New York: Macmillan, 1961.

Other books you may enjoy from Celestial Arts

The Art of Ritual *by Sydney Barbara Metrick & Renee Beck*
A guide to creating and performing personalized rituals for growth and change. The authors discuss the importance of ritual in traditional cultures, and show how to integrate it into modern life, celebrating births, achievements, special friendships, and the like. *$11.95 paper, 152 pages*

The Serpent and the Wave *by Jalaja Bonheim*
Many cultures consider dance and movement to be sacred arts, but Westerners have long igorned the power and wisdom of their bodies. This book, by a professional dancer and teacher of movement meditation, gives a fresh, new, Western approach to improving body image and gaining control through simple, well-illustrated exercises and affirmations. *$14.95 paper, 320 pages*

Choose to be Healthy *by Susan Smith Jones, Ph.D.*
The choices we make in life can greatly increase our health and happiness—this book details how to analyze one's choices about food, exercise, thought, work, and play, and then use this information to create a better, healthier life. *$9.95 paper, 252 pages*

Choose to Live Peacefully *by Susan Smith Jones, Ph.D.*
By nurturing our inner selves and living in personal peace, we can help to bring about global change. In this book, Susan Smith-Jones explores the many components of a peaceful, satisfying life—including exercise, nutrition, solitude, meditation, ritual, and environmental awareness—and shows how they can be linked to world peace. *$11.95, 320 pages*

Loving Relationships I *by Sondra Ray*
How to find, achieve, and maintain a deeper, more fulfilling relationship with your mate. *$8.95 paper, 178 pages*

Loving Relationships II *by Sondra Ray*
In this entirely new companion volume, Sondra shares her discoveries as she continues to investigate the secrets of life, love, and spirituality. *$9.95 paper, 192 pages*

...and from Ten Speed Press

Speaking of Marriage *edited by Catherine Glass*
A collection of quotes about marriage, specially designed to be a gorgeous wedding, shower, or anniversary gift. Unusual words from unexpected sources, the quotes range from playful to profound and from intimate to outrageous, with a refreshing emphasis on the positive. *$15.95 cloth, 96 pages*

**Celestial Arts/
Ten Speed Press**
Box 7123
Berkeley, CA 94707

Available from your local bookstore, or order direct from the publisher. Please include $2.50 shipping and handling for the first book, and 50 cents for each additional book. California residents include local sales tax. Write for our free complete catalog of over 400 books, posters, and tapes.

For VISA or MASTERCARD order call (800) 841-BOOK